LITURGIES AND THEIR IMPOSITIONS

John Owen

Vintage Puritan Series
GLH Publishing
Louisville, KY

Sourced from *The Works of John Owen,* Vol. XV.
Edited by William Goold. Johnstone & Hunter, London, 1851.

Republished by GLH Publishing, 2020.

ISBN:
  Paperback 978-1-64863-024-8
  Epub 978-1-64863-025-5

CONTENTS

Prefatory note. 1

Chapter I. 4
The state of the Judaical church — The liberty given by Christ; 1. From the arbitrary impositions of men; 2. From the observances and rites instituted by Moses — The continuance of their observation, in the patience and forbearance of God — Difference about them stated — Legal righteousness and legal ceremonies contended for together — The reason of it.

Chapter II. 11
The disciples of Christ taken into his own disposal — General things to be observed about gospel institutions — Their number small — Excess of men's inventions — Things instituted brought into a religious relation by the authority of Christ — That authority is none other — Suitableness in the matter of institutions, to be designed to their proper significancy — That discoverable only by infinite wisdom — Abilities given by Christ for the administration of all his institutions — The way whereby it was done, Eph. iv. 7, 8 — Several postulata laid down — The sum of the whole — State of our question in general.

Chapter III. 17
Of the Lord's prayer, and what may be concluded from thence as to the invention and imposition of liturgies in the public worship of God — The liberty whereunto Christ vindicated and wherein he left his disciples.

Chapter IV. 21
Of the worship of God by the apostles — No liturgies used by them, nor in the churches of their plantation — Argument from their practice — Reasons pleaded for the use of liturgies: disabilities of church officers for gospel administration to the edification of the church; uniformity in the worship of God — The practice of the apostles as to these pretences considered — Of other impositions — The rule given by the apostles — Of the liturgies falsely ascribed unto some of them.

Chapter V. 28
The practice of the churches in the first three centuries as to forms of public worship — No set forms of liturgies used by them — The silence of the first writers concerning them — Some testimonies against them.

Chapter VI. 34
The pretended antiquity of liturgies disproved — The most ancient — Their variety — Canons of councils about forms of church administrations — The reasons pleaded in the justification of the first invention of liturgies answered — Their progress and end.

Chapter VII. 45
The question stated — First argument against the composing and imposing of liturgies — Arbitrary additions to the worship of God rejected — Liturgies not appointed by God — Made necessary in their imposition, and a part of the worship of God — Of circumstances of worship — Instituted adjuncts of worship not circumstances — Circumstances of actions, as such, not circumstances of worship — Circumstances commanded made parts of worship — Prohibitions of additions produced, considered, applied.

Chapter VIII. 58
Of the authority needful for the constituting and ordering of any thing that is to have relation to God and his worship — Of the power and authority of civil magistrates — The power imposing the liturgy — The formal reason of religious obedience — Use of the liturgy an act of civil, not religious obedience, Matt. xxviii. 20 — No rule to judge of what is meet in the worship of God, but his word.

Chapter IX. 64
Argument second — Necessary use of the liturgy exclusive of the use of the means appointed by Christ for the edification of his church.

Chapter X. 70
Other considerations about the imposition of liturgies.

PREFATORY NOTE.

It deserves attention that this pamphlet, with its humble title, "A Discourse concerning Liturgies," etc., and printed anonymously in 1662, contains the judgment of our author in regard to measures which gave rise to most important events in the ecclesiastical history of England. It is an argument against the liturgy, the imposition of which obliged nearly two thousand clergy of the Church of England to resign their livings rather than sacrifice a good conscience.

On the Restoration, the Book of Common Prayer had been resumed in the royal chapel at Whitehall; it was ordained to be read in the House of Peers; and before the year closed, some of the parochial clergy, who scrupled to use it, were prosecuted according to the laws in force before the civil war.

As many leading Presbyterians, however, had been favourable to the Restoration, the Court could not afford at first to come to an open rupture with them, and accordingly, in 1661, a conference was appointed between twelve bishops and an equal number of Presbyterian ministers, with instructions to revise the Book of Common Prayer, so as to bring it into conformity with the religious convictions of both parties, and establish peace and unity in the church. This conference, however, after long and keen debate, broke up without any good results.

The Convocation was then ordered to revise the liturgy. The changes made on it were not such as to relieve the consciences of the Presbyterians; but, nevertheless, as revised by the Convocation, it was adopted by Parliament, and ratified by the Act for Uniformity in the Prayers and Ceremonies of the Church of England. This act, designed, according to Burnet, to make the terms of conformity stricter than before, passed the House of Commons by a majority of 186 to 180, The House of

Lords endeavoured to abate the stringency of some of its provisions, but, supported by the Court, the majority in the Lower House effectually resisted the modifications proposed. The bill passed the House of Peers by a small majority, and received the royal assent on 19th May 1662. The act required all ministers to announce publicly their adherence to the liturgy, and to subscribe a declaration that it was unlawful, upon any pretence, to take arms against the king, or to endeavour any change in the government of church or state. No person, moreover, according to the act, could hold a benefice or administer the Lord's supper unless he was episcopally ordained. Fines, imprisonment, and the forfeiture of their livings, were the penalties to be inflicted on those who could not yield compliance with the law. The act took effect on the 24th of August, and nearly two thousand devout and faithful pastors were then expelled from the Church of England.

The chief merit of the following tract can only be understood in the light of these exciting events. From some expressions in it, it must have been written while the contest prevailed, and before the liturgy was actually imposed; and yet the whole argument is conducted in perfect temper, and the readers of Owen might fail to bear in mind that he is discussing a question which was stirring English society to its depths, and involved consequences unparalleled in English history. The treatise has all the weight and gravity of a judicial decision. The author, rising above petty details, expends his strength in proof that the *imposition* of a liturgy by civil enactment is an interference with the authority of Christ; and, unwilling to heighten the asperities of the prevailing controversy, he excludes from discussion the character of the English liturgy, and confines himself to the abstract question, as to the lawfulness of enforcing it on the conscience as essential to divine worship. It is the more honourable to Owen that he should have exerted himself against the imposition of the liturgy, when it is remembered that as at this time he held no living in the church, he could not suffer under the Act of Uniformity, and the measures of the Court were directed against the Presbyterians rather than the Independents. Orme remarks of this production and its subject, "The principle which these forms of human composition involve is of vast importance; and I know not where, in so small a compass, this principle is so well stated and so ably opposed as in this work." — ED.

CHAPTER I.

The state of the Judaical church — The liberty given by Christ; 1. From the arbitrary impositions of men; 2. From the observances and rites instituted by Moses — The continuance of their observation, in the patience and forbearance of God — Difference about them stated — Legal righteousness and legal ceremonies contended for together — The reason of it.

ALTHOUGH our present inquiry be merely after one part of instituted worship under the gospel, and the due performance of it according to the mind of God, yet, there being a communication of some light to be obtained from the turning over of that worship from the Mosaical to the care and practice of the evangelical church, we shall look a little back unto it as therein stated; hoping thereby to make way for our clearer progress. What was the state of the church of God amongst the Jews as to instituted worship, when our blessed Saviour came to make the last and perfect discovery of his mind and will, is manifest both from the appointment of that worship in the law of Moses, and the practice of it remarked in the gospel. That the rites and ordinances of the worship in the church observed, were from the original in their nature *carnal*, and for the number *many*, on both accounts *burdensome* and grievous to the worshippers, the Scripture frequently declares. Howbeit, the teachers and rulers of the church, being grown wholly carnal in their spirits, and placing their only glory in their yoke, not being able to see to the end of the things that were to be done away, had increased those institutions, both in number and weight, with sundry inventions of their own; which, by their authority, they made necessary to be observed by their disciples. In an equal practice of these divine institutions and human inventions did our Lord Jesus Christ find the generality of the church at his coming in the flesh. The former, being to continue in force until the time of reformation, at his resurrection from the dead, should come, both by his practice and his teaching, as a minister of Circumcision, he confirmed and pressed frequently on the consciences of men, from the authority of the Law-maker. The latter he utterly rejected, as introduced in a high derogation from the perfection of the law, and the honour of Him whose prerogative it is to be the sole lawgiver of his church, — the only fountain and disposer of his own worship. And this was the first dawning of liberty that, with the rising of this Day-star, did appear to the burdened and languishing consciences of men. He freed them, by his teaching, from the bondage of Pharisaical, arbitrary impositions, delivering their consciences from subjection to any thing in the worship of God but his own immediate authority. For it may not be supposed that, when he recommended unto his hearers an attendance unto the teaching of the scribes and Pharisees, with an injunction to obey their directions, that he intended aught but those commands which they gave from Him, and according to his mind, whose fear they did outwardly profess; seeing that, both in general and particular, he did himself condemn their traditions and impositions, giving out a rule of liberty from them unto others in his own constant practice. Yea, and whereas he would do *civil* things in their own nature indifferent, whereunto he was by no righteous law obliged, to avoid the offence of any which he saw might follow, Matt. xvii. 27, yet would he not practise or give countenance unto, nay, nor abstain from condemning of, any of their ecclesiastical self-invented observances, though he saw them offended and scandalized at him, and was by others informed no less, chap. xv. 12–14; confirming his practice with that standing rule concerning all things relating to the worship of God, "Every plant which my heavenly Father hath not planted shall be rooted up." But he is yet farther to carry on the work of giving liberty to all the disciples, that he might take them into a subjection to himself and his own authority only. The Aaronical priesthood being the hinge on which the whole ceremonial worship turned, so that upon a change thereof the obligation of the law unto that worship, or any part of it, was necessarily to cease, our blessed Saviour, in his death and oblation, entering upon the office, and actually discharging the great duty of his priesthood, did virtually put an end to the whole obligation of the first institution of Mosaical worship. In his death was the procurement of the liberty of his disciples completely finished, as unto conscience; the *supposed* obligation of men's traditions, and the *real* obligation of Mosaical institutions, being by him (the first as a prophet in his teaching, the last as a priest in his offering) dissolved and taken away. From that day all the disciples of Christ were taken under his immediate lordship, and made free to the end of the from all obligations in conscience unto any thing in the worship of God but what is of his own institution and command.

This dissolution of the obligation of "the law of commandments contained in ordinances," being declared by his apostles and disciples, became a matter of great difference and debate amongst the Jews, to whom the gospel was first preached. Those who before had slain him, in pursuit of their own charge, that he would bring in such an alteration in the worship of God as was now divulged, were many of them exceedingly enraged at this new doctrine, and had their prejudices against him and his way much increased, — hating indeed the light, because their deeds were evil. These being obstinately bent to seek after righteousness (as it were, at least) by the works of the law, contended for their ceremonial works as one of the best stakes in their hedge, in whose observance they placed their chiefest confidence of their acceptance with God. But this is not all: many who, falling under powerful convictions of his doctrine and miracles, believed on him did yet pertinaciously adhere to their old ceremonial worship. Partly for want of clear light and understanding in the doctrine of the person and office of the Messiah; partly through the power of unspeakable prejudices which influenced their minds in reference to those rites which, being from of old observed by their forefathers, derived their original from God himself (much the most noble pleas and pretences that ever any of the sons of men had to insist upon for a subjection to such a yoke as indeed had lost all power to oblige them); they were very desirous to mix the observance of them with obedience unto those institutions which they, through the Lord Jesus, had superadded to them.

Things being thus stated amongst the Jews, God having a great work to accomplish among and upon them in a short time, would not have the effect of it turn upon this hinge merely; and therefore, in his infinite wisdom and condescension, waived the whole contest for a season. For whereas, within the space of forty years or thereabout, he was to call and gather out from the body, by the preaching gospel, his remnant according to the election of grace, and to leave the rest inexcusable, — thereby visibly glorifying his justice in their temporal and eternal ruin, — it pleased him, in a way of connivance and forbearance, to continue unto that people an allowance of the observation of their old worship until the time appointed for its utter removal and actual casting away should come. Though the original obligation on conscience, from the first institution of their ceremonies, was taken away, yet hence arose a new necessity of the observation of them, even in them who were acquainted with the dissolution of that obligation, — namely, from the offence and scandal of them to whom their observance was providentially indulged. On this account the disciples of Christ (and the apostles themselves) continued in a promiscuous observation of Mosaical institutions with the rest of the body of that people, until the appointed season of the utter rejection and destruction of the apostate churches was come. Hence many of the ancients affirm that James the Less, living at Jerusalem in great reputation with all the people for his sanctity and righteousness, was not, to the very time of his martyrdom, known to be a Christian; which had been utterly impossible had he totally abstained from communion with them in legal worship. Neither had that old controversy about the feast of the passover any other rise or spring than the mistake of some, who thought John had observed it as a Christian, who kept it only as a Judaical feast among the Jews: whence the tradition ran strong that he observed it with them on the fourteenth day of the month; which precise time others, turning it into a Christian observation, thought meet to lay aside.

Things being thus stated, in the connivance and forbearance of God, among the Jews, some of them, not contented to use the indulgence, granted to them in mere patience, for the ends before mentioned, began sedulously to urge the Mosaical rites upon all the Gentiles that were turned unto God; so making, upon the matter, the preaching of the gospel to be but a new way of proselyting men unto Judaism. For the most part, it appears that it was not any mistake or unacquaintedness with the liberty brought in by Christ that made them engage in this quarrel for Moses; but that indeed, being themselves carnal, and, notwithstanding the outward name of Christ, seeking yet for righteousness by the law, they esteemed the observation of the ceremonies indispensably necessary unto salvation. This gave occasion unto Paul, unto whom the apostleship of the Gentiles was in a special manner committed, to lay open the whole mystery of that liberty given by Christ to his disciples from the law of Moses; as also the pernicious effects which its observance would produce, upon those principles which were pressed by the Judaical zealots. Passing by the peculiar dispensation of God towards the whole nation of the Jews, wherein the Gentile believers were not concerned; as also that determination of the case of scandal made at Jerusalem, Acts xv., and the temporary rule of condescension as to the abridgment of liberty in some particulars agreed unto thereupon; he fully declares that the time of the appointment was come, that there was no more power in the law of their institutions to bind the consciences of men, and that it was not in the power of all the men in the world to impose the observation of them, or any like unto them, upon anyone, though the meanest of the disciples of Jesus Christ. The mind of Christ in this matter being fully made known, and the liberty of his disciples vindicated, various effects in the minds of men ensued thereupon. Those who were in their inward principle themselves carnal, notwithstanding their outward profession of the gospel, delighting in and resting on an outward ceremonious worship, continued to oppose him with violence and fury. Those who with the profession of the Lord Christ had also received the Spirit of Christ, and were by him instructed, as in the perfection of righteousness, so in the beauty and excellency of the worship of the gospel, rejoiced greatly in the grace and privilege of the purchased liberty. After many contests, this controversy was buried in the ruins of the city and temple, when the main occasion was utterly taken away.

By these degrees were the disciples of Christ put into a complete actual possession of that liberty which he had preached to them, and purchased for them. Being first delivered from any conscientious subjection to the institutions of men, and then to the temporary institutions of God which concerned them not, they were left in a dependence on and subjection unto himself alone, as to all things concerning worship; in which state he will assuredly continue and preserve them to the end of the world, under the guidance and direction of those rules for the use of their liberty which he has left in his word. But yet the principle of the difference before mentioned, which is fixed in the minds of men by nature, did not die together with the controversy that mainly issued from it. We may trace it effectually exerting itself in succeeding ages. As ignorance of the righteousness of God, with a desire to establish their own, did in any take place, so also did endeavours after an outward, ceremonious worship: for these things do mutually further and strengthen each other; and commonly proportionable unto men's darkness in the mystery of the righteousness of God in Christ is their zeal for a worldly sanctuary and carnal ordinances. And such hath been the force and efficacy of these combined principles in the minds of carnal men, that, under the profession of Christianity, they reduced things (in the Papacy) to the very state and condition wherein they were in Judaism at the time of reformation; the main principle in the one and the other church, in the apostasy, being righteousness and an insupportable yoke of ceremonious observances in the worship of God. And generally, in others the same principles of legal righteousness and a ceremonious worship have prevalency in a just proportion, the latter being regulated by the former; and where by any means the former is everted, the latter for the most part falls of its own accord; yea, though riveted in the minds of men by other prejudices also. Hence when the soul of a sinner is effectually wrought upon, by the preaching of the gospel, to renounce himself and his own righteousness, and, being truly humbled for sin, to receive the Lord Christ by faith, as "made unto him of God wisdom, righteousness, sanctification, and redemption," there needs, for the most part, little arguing to dissuade him from resting in or laying weight upon an outside, pompous worship; but he is immediately sensible of a delivery from its yoke, which he freely embraceth. And the reason hereof is, because that good Spirit by whom he is enabled to believe and receive the Lord Jesus Christ, gives him also an acquaintance with, and an experience of, the excellency, glory, and beauty of that spiritual communion with God in Christ whereunto believers are called in the gospel; which discovers the emptiness and uselessness of all which before, perhaps, he admired and delighted in: for "where the Spirit of Christ is, there is liberty." And these things, — of seeking a righteousness in Christ alone, and delighting in spiritual communion with God, exercising itself only in the ways of his own appointment, — do inseparably proceed from the same Spirit of Christ, as those before mentioned from the same principle of self and flesh.

CHAPTER II.

The disciples of Christ taken into his own disposal — General things to be observed about gospel institutions — Their number small — Excess of men's inventions — Things instituted brought into a religious relation by the authority of Christ — That authority is none other — Suitableness in the matter of institutions, to be designed to their proper significancy — That discoverable only by infinite wisdom — Abilities given by Christ for the administration of all his institutions — The way whereby it was done, Eph. iv. 7, 8 — Several postulata laid down — The sum of the whole — State of our question in general.

WE have brought unto and left the disciples of Jesus Christ in the hand and sole disposal of him, their Lord and Master, as to all things which concern the worship of God; and how he hath disposed of them we are in the next place to consider. Now, he being the Head, Lord, and only Lawgiver of his church, coming from the bosom of his Father to make the last revelation of his mind and will, was to determine and appoint that worship of God in and by himself which was to continue to the end of the world. It belongeth not unto our purpose to consider distinctly and apart all the several institutions which by him were ordained. We shall only observe some things concerning them in general, that will be of use in our progress, and so proceed to the consideration of that particular about which we are in disquisition of his mind and will. The worship of God is either moral and internal, or external and of sovereign or arbitrary institution. The former we do not now consider; nor was the ancient, original, fundamental obligation unto it altered or dissolved in the least by the Lord Christ. It was as unto superadded institutions of outward worship, which have their foundation and reason in sovereign will and pleasure, that he took his disciples into his own disposal, discharging them from all obligations to aught else whatever but only what he should appoint. Concerning these, some few considerations will lead us to what in this discourse we principally intend. And the first is, *That they were few, and easy to be observed*. It was his will and pleasure that the faith and love of his disciples should, in some few instances, be exercised in a willing, ready subjection to the impositions of his wisdom and authority; and their service herein he doth fully recompense, by rendering those his institutions blessedly useful to their spiritual advantage. But he would not burden them with observances, either for nature or number, like or comparable unto them from which he purchased liberty. And herein hath the practice of succeeding ages put an excellent lustre upon his love and tenderness. For whereas he is the Lord of his church, to whom the consciences of his disciples are in an unquestionable subjection, and who can give power and efficacy to his institutions to make them useful to their souls, yet some of their fellow-servants came, I know not how, to apprehend themselves enabled to impose arbitrarily their appointments, reasons seeming good to their wisdom, they might have been considered moderate if they had not given above ten commandments for his one. Bellarmine tells us, indeed, that the laws and institutions of the church that absolutely bind all Christians, so that they omit their observation, are upon the matter but four, — namely, to observe the fasts of Lent and Ember-weeks, to keep the holy days, confession once a year, and to communicate at Easter, De Rom. Pontif., lib. iv. cap. 18. But whereas they double the number of the sacred ceremonies instituted by Christ, and have every one of them a greater number of subservient observations attending on them, so he must be a stranger to their councils, canon-laws, and practices, that can believe his insinuation.

Again: as the institutions and ordinances of Christ in the outward worship of God, whose sole foundation was in his will and pleasure, were few, and easy to be observed, being brought into a relation of worship unto God by virtue of his institution and command, without which no one thing in their kind can do so more than another; so they were, for the matter of them, such as he knew had *an aptness to be serviceable unto the significancy* whereunto they were appointed by him, which nothing but infinite wisdom can judge of. And this eternally severs them from all things of men's invention, either to the same purpose, or in the same way to be used. For as whatever they shall appoint in the worship of God can have no significancy at all, as unto any spiritual end, for want of a Christ-like authority in their institution, which alone can add that significancy to them which in themselves, without such an appointment, they have not; so they themselves, want wisdom to choose the things which have any fitness or aptitude to be used for that end, if the authority were sufficient to introduce with them such a significancy. There is nothing they can in this kind fix upon, but as good reason as any they are able to tender, for the proof of their expedience unto the end proposed to them, will be produced to prove them meet for a quite other signification and purpose, and the contrary unto them, at least things diverse to them, be asserted with as fair pretences, as meet to be used in their place and room.

But that which we principally shall observe, in and about Christ's institutions of gospel worship, is the provision that he made for the administration of it acceptably unto God. It is of the instituted worship of his public assemblies that we treat. The chiefest acts and parts thereof may be referred to these three heads:— *preaching of the word, administration of the sacraments, and the exercise of discipline;* all to be performed with prayer and thanksgiving. The rule for the administration of these things, so far as they are purely of his institution, he gave his disciples in his appointment of them. Persons, also, he designed to the regular administration of these his holy things in the assemblies of his saints, — namely, pastors and teachers, — to endure to the end of the world, after those of an extraordinary employment under him were to cease. It remaineth, then, to consider how the persons appointed by him unto the administration of these holy things in his assemblies, and so to the discharge of the whole public worship of God, should be enabled thereunto, so as the end by him aimed at, of the edification of his disciples and the glory of God, might be attained. Two ways there are whereby this may be done: First, By such spiritual abilities for the discharge and performance of this whole work as will answer the mind of Christ therein, and so serve for the end proposed. Secondly, By the prescription of a form of words, whose reading and pronunciation in these administrations should outwardly serve as to all the ends of the prayer and thanksgiving required in them, which they do contain. It is evident that our Saviour fixed on the former way; what he hath done as to the latter, or what his mind is concerning it, we shall afterward inquire.

For the first, as in many other places, so signally in one, the apostle acquaints us with the course he has taken, and the provision that he hath made — namely, Eph. iv. 7, 8, 11-13: "Unto every one of us is given grace, according to the measure of the gift of Christ. Wherefore he saith, When he ascended up on high, he led captivity captive, and gave gifts unto men. And he gave some, apostles; and some, prophets; some, evangelists; and some, pastors and teachers; for the perfecting of the saints, for the work of the ministry, for the edifying of the body of Christ: till we all come in the unity of the faith, and of the knowledge of the Son of God, unto a perfect man, unto the measure of the stature of the fulness of Christ," etc. The thing aimed at is, the bringing of all the saints and disciples of Christ, the whole church, to that measure and perfection of grace which Christ hath assigned to them in this world, that may be meet for himself to receive in glory. The means whereby this is to be done and effected is, the faithful and regular discharge of the work of the ministry; unto which the administration of all his ordinances and institutions doth confessedly belong. That this work may be discharged in an orderly manner to the end mentioned, he has granted unto his church the offices mentioned, to be executed by persons variously called thereunto, according to his mind and will.

The only inquiry remaining is, how these persons shall be enabled for the discharge of their office, and so accomplishment of the work of the ministry? This, he declares, is by the communication of grace and spiritual gifts from heaven unto them by Christ himself. Here lieth the spring of all that followeth, — the care hereof he hath taken upon himself unto the end of the world. He that enabled the shoulders of the Levites to bear the ark of old, and their arms to slay the sacrifices, without which natural strength those carnal ordinances could not have been observed (nor was the ark to be carried for a supply of defect of ability in the Levites), hath, upon their removal, and the institution of the spiritual worship of the gospel, undertaken to supply the administrators of it with spiritual strength and abilities for the discharge of their work, allowing them supply of the defect of which he hath taken upon himself to perform. I suppose, then, these ensuing will seem but reasonable postulata:—

1. That the means which Jesus Christ hath appointed for the attaining of any end, is every way sufficient for that purpose whereunto it is so appointed. His wisdom exacts our consent to this proposition.

2. That what he hath taken upon himself to perform unto the end of the world, and promised so to do, that he will accomplish accordingly. Here his faithfulness requires our assent.

3. That the communication of spiritual gifts and graces to the ministers of the gospel, is the provision that Christ hath made for the discharge of the work of their ministry, unto the edification of his body. This lies plain in the text.

4. That the exercise and use of those gifts, in all those administrations for which they are bestowed, are expected and required by him. The nature of the thing itself, with innumerable testimonies, confirm this truth also.

5. That it is derogatory to the glory, honour, and faithfulness of the Lord Jesus Christ, to affirm that he ceaseth to bestow gifts for the work of the ministry, whilst he continueth and requireth the exercise and discharge of that work. What hath befallen men, or doth yet befall them, through the wretched sloth, darkness, and unbelief, which their wilful neglect of dependence on him, or of stirring up or improving of what they do receive from him, and the mischiefs that have accrued to the church by the intrusion of such persons into the place and office of the ministry as were never called nor appointed by him thereunto, are not to be imputed unto any failing on his part, in his promise of dispensing the gifts mentioned to the end of the

world. Of which several positions we shall have some use in our farther progress.

Our Lord Jesus Christ, then, having delivered his disciples from the yoke of Mosaical institutions, which lay upon them from of old; as also from being entangled in their consciences by or from any inventions of men imposed on them; giving them rules for the practice of the liberty whereunto by him they were vindicated, taking them for the future into his own sole disposal in all things concerning the worship of God, he appoints, in his sovereign authority, both the ordinances which he will have alone observed in his church, and the persons by whom they are to be administered; [and] furnishing them with spiritual abilities to that end and purpose, promising his presence with them to the end of the world, commands them to set such, in his name and strength, in the way and unto the work that he hath allotted to them.

That, now, which on this foundation we are farther to inquire into is, whether, over and above what we have recounted, our Saviour hath appointed, or by any ways given allowance unto, the framing of a stinted form of prayers and praises, to be read and used by the administrators of his ordinances in their administration of them? or whether the prescription and imposing of such a form or liturgy upon those who minister in the church, in the name and authority of Christ, be not contrary to his mind, and cross to his whole design for perpetuating of his institutions to the end of the world, in due order and manner? And this we shall do, and withal discover the rise and progress which such liturgies have had and made in the church of God.

CHAPTER III.

Of the Lord's prayer, and what may be concluded from thence as to the invention and imposition of liturgies in the public worship of God — The liberty whereunto Christ vindicated and wherein he left his disciples.

THE first plea used to give countenance unto the composing and imposing of liturgies is taken from that act of our Saviour himself, who, upon the request of his disciples, composed for them a form of prayer; which, being recorded in the gospel, is said to have the force of an institution, rendering the observation or use of that form a necessary duty unto all believers to the end of the world. And this plea is strengthened by a discovery which some learned men say they have made, — namely, that our blessed Saviour composed this form, which he delivered to his disciples, out of such other forms as were then in ordinary use among the Jews; whereby, they say, he confirmed that practice of prescribing forms of prayer among them, and recommended the same course of proceeding, by his so doing, unto his disciples. Now, though it be very hard to discover how, upon a supposition that all which is thus suggested is the very truth, any thing can be hence concluded to the justification of the practice of imposing liturgies, now inquired into; yet, that there may be no pretence left unto a plea, though never so weak and infirm, of such an extract as this lays claim unto, it will be necessary to consider the severals of it. It is generally apprehended that our Saviour, in his prescription of that form of prayer unto his disciples, did aim at two things:— 1. That they might have a summary symbol of all the most excellent things they were to ask of God in his name, and so a rule of squaring all their desires and supplications by. This end all universally concur in; and therefore Matthew, considering the doctrinal nature of it, gives it a place in the first recorded sermon of our Saviour, by way of anticipation, and mentions it not when he comes to the time wherein it was really first delivered by him. 2. For their benefit and advantage, together with other intercessions that they should also use the repetition of those words, as a prescript form wherein he had comprised the matter of their requests and petitions. About this latter all men are not agreed in their judgments, whether indeed our Saviour had this aim in it or no. Many learned men suppose that it was a supply of a rule and standard of things to be prayed for, without prescribing to them the use or rehearsal of that form of words, that he aimed at. Of this number are Musculus, Grotius, and Cornelius à Lapide, with many others; but it may suffice to intimate, that some of all sorts are so minded. But we shall not, in the case in hand, make use of any principle so far obnoxious unto common prejudice as experience proves that opinion of these learned men to be. Let it, therefore, be taken for granted that our Saviour did command that form to be repeated by his disciples, and let us then consider what will regularly ensue thereupon. Our Saviour at that time was minister of the Circumcision, and taught the doctrine of the gospel under and with the observation of all the worship of the Judaical church. He was not yet glorified, and so the Spirit was not as yet given; I mean that Spirit which he promised unto his disciples to enable them to perform all the worship of God by him required at their hands, whereof we have before spoken. That, then, which the Lord Jesus prescribed unto his disciples, for their present practice in the worship of God, seems to have belonged unto the economy of the Old Testament. Now, to argue from the prescription of, and outward helps for, the performance of the worship of God under the Old Testament, unto a necessity of the like or the same under the New, is upon the matter to deny that Christ is ascended on high, and to have given spiritual gifts unto men eminently distinct from and above those given out by him under the Judaical pedagogy. However, their boldness seems unwarrantable, if not intolerable, who, to serve their own ends, upon this prescription of his, do affirm that our Lord Jesus composed this form out of such as were then in common use among the Jews. For as the proof of their assertion which they

Chapter III.

insist on, — namely, the finding of some of the things expressed in it, or petitions of it, in the writings of the Jews, the eldest whereof is some hundreds of years younger than this prayer itself, — is most weak and contemptible; so the affirmation itself is exceeding derogatory to the glory and honour of his wisdom, assigning unto him a work so unnecessary and trivial as would scarce become a man of ordinary prudence and authority. But yet, to carry on the work in hand, let it be supposed that our Saviour did command that form of prayer out of such as were then customarily used among the Jews (which is false, and asserted without any colour of proof); also, that he prescribed it as a form to be repeated by his disciples (which we have shown many very eminently learned men to deny); and that, though he prescribed it as a minister to the Judaical church, and to his disciples whilst members of that church, under the economy of the Old Testament, not having as yet received the Spirit and gifts of the New, yet that he did it for the use and observance of his disciples to the end of the world, and that not as to the objective regulation of their prayers, but as to the repetition of the words; yet it doth not appear how, from all these concessions, any argument can be drawn to the composition and imposition of liturgies, whose rise and nature we are inquiring after: for it is certain that our Saviour gives this direction for the end which he intends in it, not primarily as to the public worship of the assemblies of his disciples, but as to the guidance of every individual saint in his private devotion, Matt. vi. 6–8. Now, from a direction given unto private persons, as to their private deportment in the discharge of any religious duty, to argue unto a prescription of the whole worship of God in public assemblies is not safe. But, that we may hear the argument drawn from this act of our Saviour speak out all that it hath to offer, let us add this also to the fore-mentioned presumptions that our Saviour hath appointed and ordained, that in the assemblies of his disciples, in his worship by him required, they who administer in his name in and to the church should repeat the words of this prayer, though not peculiarly suited to any one of his institutions: what will thence be construed to ensue? Why, then, it is supposed that this will follow, — That it is not only lawful, but the duty of some men to compose other forms, a hundred times as many, suited in their judgment to the due administration of all ordinances of worship is particular, imposing them on the evangelical administrations of those ordinances to be read by them, with a severe interdiction of the use of any other prayers in those administrations. Bellarmine, De Pont. Rom., lib. iv. cap. 16, argues for the necessity of the observation of rites indifferent, when once commanded by the church, from the necessity of the observation of baptism, in itself a thing indifferent, after it was commanded by Christ. Some think not to dispute, but blaspheme. Nor is the inference before mentioned of any other complexion. When it shall be made to appear, that whatever it was lawful for the Lord Christ to do and to prescribe to his church and disciples, in reference to the worship of God, the same, or any thing of the like nature, it is lawful for men to do, under the pretence of their being invested with the authority of the church, or any else whatever, then some colour will be given to this argument; which being raised on the tottering suppositions before mentioned, ends in that which seems to deserve a harder name than at present we shall affix to it.

And this is the state and condition wherein the disciples of Christ were left by himself, without the least intimation of any other impositions in the worship of God to be laid upon them. Nor in any thing, or by any act of his, did he intimate the necessity or lawful use of any such liturgies as these which we are inquiring after, or prescribed and limited forms of prayers or praises, to be used or read in public administration of evangelical institutions; but indeed made provision rendering all such prescriptions useless, and (because they cannot be made use of but by rejection of the provision himself by made) unlawful.

CHAPTER IV.

Of the worship of God by the apostles — No liturgies used by them, nor in the churches of their plantation — Argument from their practice — Reasons pleaded for the use of liturgies: disabilities of church officers for gospel administration to the edification of the church; uniformity in the worship of God — The practice of the apostles as to these pretences considered — Of other impositions — The rule given by the apostles — Of the liturgies falsely ascribed unto some of them.

OUR next inquiry is after the practice of the apostles, — the best interpretation of the mind of the Lord Jesus Christ as to the "agenda" of the church, or what he would have done therein in the worship of God, and how. That one end of their being furnished with the Spirit of Christ, was the right and due administration of his ordinances in his church, to the edification of his disciples, I suppose will not be denied. By virtue of his assistance, and the gifts from him received, they discharged this part of their duty accordingly. That they used any liturgies in the church-worship, wherein they went at any time before the disciples, cannot with any colour of proof be pretended. The Scripture gives us an account of many of their prayers, — of none that were a repetition of a form. If any such were used by them, how came the memory of them utterly to perish from off the earth? Some, indeed, of the ancients say that they used the Lord's prayer in the consecration of the eucharist; which by others is denied, being in itself improbable, and the testimonies weak that are produced in behalf of its assertion. But, as hath been showed, the use of that prayer no way concerns the present question. There are no more Christs but one: "To us there is one Lord Jesus Christ." For him who hath affirmed that it is likely they used forms of prayer and homilies composed for them by St Peter, I suppose he must fetch his evidence out of the same authors that he used who affirmed that Jesus Christ himself went up and down singing mass!

The practice, then, of the apostles is not, as far as I know, by any sober and learned persons controverted in this matter. They administered the holy thing of the gospel by virtue of the holy gifts they had received. But they were apostles. The inquiry is, what directions and commands they gave unto the bishops or pastors of the churches which they planted, that they might know how to behave themselves in the house and worship of God. Whatever they might do in the discharge of their duty, by virtue of their extraordinary gifts, yet the case might be much otherwise with them who were intrusted with ordinary ministerial gifts only. But we do not find that they made any distinction in this matter between themselves and others; for as the care of all the churches was on them, the duties whereof they were to discharge by virtue of the gifts they had received, according to their commission empowering them thereunto, so to the bishops of particular churches they gave charge to attend unto the administration of the holy things in them, by virtue of the gifts they had received to that purpose, according to the limits of their commission. And upon a supposition that the apostles were enabled to discharge all gospel administrations to the edification of the church, by virtue of the gifts they had received, which those who were to come after them in the performance of the same duties not be enabled unto, it cannot be imagined but that they have provided a supply for that want and defect themselves, and not have left the church halt and maimed to the cure of those whose weakness and unfitness for the duty was its disease. So, then neither did the apostles of our Lord Jesus Christ use any liturgies, in the sense spoken of, in their administration of the worship instituted by him in his church, nor did they prescribe or command any such to the churches, or their officers that were planted in them; nor by any thing intimate the usefulness of any such liturgy, or form of public worship, as after ages found out and used.

Thus far, then, is the liberty given by Christ unto his church preserved entire; and the request seems not immodest that is made for the continuance of it. When men cry to God for the liberty in his worship which was left unto them by Christ and his apostles, he will hear, though their fellow-servants should be deaf to the requests made unto them; and truly they must have a great confidence in their own wisdom and sufficiency, who will undertake to appoint, and impose on others, the observation of things in the worship of God which neither our Lord Jesus nor his apostles did appoint or impose.

Two things are principally pretended as grounds of the imposition of public liturgies:— First, The disability of the present ministers of churches to celebrate and administer the ordinances of the gospel, to the honour of God and edification of the church, without the use of them. Secondly, The great importance of uniformity in the worship of God, not possibly to be attained but by virtue of this expedient. I desire to know whether these arguments did occur to the consideration of the apostles or no. If they shall say they did, I desire to know why they did not make upon them the provision now judged necessary; and whether those that so do, do not therein prefer their wisdom and care for the churches of God unto the wisdom and care of the apostles. If it shall be said, that the bishops or pastors of the churches in their days had abilities for the discharge of the whole work of the ministry without this relief, so that the apostles had no need to make any such supply, I desire to know from whom they had these abilities. If it be said that they had them from Jesus Christ, I then shall yet also farther ask, whether ordinary bishops or pastors had any other gifts from Jesus Christ but what he promised to bestow on ordinary bishops and pastors of his churches? It seems to me that he bestowed no more upon them than he promised to bestow, — namely, gifts for the work of the ministry, with an especial regard to that outward condition of his churches whereunto by his providence they were disposed. It will, then, in the next place, be inquired whether the Lord Jesus Christ promised to give any other gifts to the ordinary bishops and pastors of the churches in those days than he promised to all such officers in his church to the end of the world? If this appear to be the state of things, that the promise by virtue whereof they received those gifts and abilities for the discharge of their duty which rendered the prescription of liturgies needless, as to the first ground of them pretended, did and doth equally respect all that succeed in the same office and duty, according to the mind and will of Christ, unto the end of the world, is not the pretended necessity derogatory to the glory of the faithfulness of Jesus Christ, as plainly intimating that he doth not continue to fulfil his promise; or at least a full declaration of men's unbelief, that they do not nor will depend upon him for the accomplishment of the same? Thus the first pretended ground of the necessary use of such liturgies as we speak of endeth in a reflection upon the honour of our Lord Jesus, or a publication of their own unbelief and apostasy.

The second is like the former. It will not, I suppose, be denied but that the apostles took care for the unity of the churches, and for that uniformity in the worship of God which is acceptable unto him. Evidence lies so full unto it in their writings that it cannot be denied. Great weight everywhere they lay upon this duty of the churches, and propose unto them the ways whereby it may be done, with multiplied commands and exhortations to attend unto them. Whence is it, then, that they never once intimate any thing of that which is now pressed as the only medium for the attaining of that end? It cannot but seem strange to some, that this should be the only expedient for that uniformity which is acceptable unto God, and yet not once come into the thoughts of any of the apostles of Christ, so as to be commended unto the churches for that purpose. Considering the many treacheries that are in the hearts of men, and the powerful workings of unbelief under the most solemn outward professions, I fear it will appear at the last day, that the true rise of most of the impositions on the consciences of men, which on various pretences are practised in the world, is from the secret thoughts that either Christ doth not take that care of his churches, nor make that supply unto them of spiritual abilities for the work of the ministry, which he did in the days of old; or that men are now grown wiser than the apostles, and those who succeeded them in the administration of the things of God, and so are able to make better provision for attaining the end they professedly aimed at than they knew how to do.

Chapter IV.

The heathen, I confess, thought forms of prayer to be a means of preserving a uniformity in their religious worship. Hence they had a solemn form for every public action; yea, for those orations which the magistrates had unto the people. So Livius informs us, that when Sp. Posthumius the consul was to speak unto the people about the wickednesses that were perpetrated by many under the pretence of some Bacchanalian superstition, he gave them an account of the usefulness of the "solenne precationis carmen," which he had recited to keep out and prevent such differences about their religion as were then fallen out, lib. xxix. 15: "Concione advocata cum solenne carmen precationis, quod præfari, priusquam populum alloquantur, magistratus solent, peregisset consul, ita cœpit: 'Nulli unquam concioni, Quirites, tam non solum apta, sed etiam necessaria, hæc solennis Deorum comprecatio fuit, quæ nos admoneret, hos esse Deos, quos colere, venerari, precarique majores vestri instituissent, non illos,'" etc. But I hope we shall not prefer their example and wisdom before that of our Lord Christ and his apostles.

Were prejudices removed, and self-interests laid out of the way, a man would think there were not much more necessity for the determination of this difference. Christ and his apostles, with the apostolical churches, knew no such liturgies. At least it seems, as was said, not an unreasonable request, to ask humbly and peaceably at the hands of any of the sons of men, that they would be pleased to allow unto ministers of the gospel that are sound in the faith, and known so to be, who will willingly submit the trial of their ministerial abilities to the judgment of any who are taught of God, and enabled to discern of them aright, that liberty in the worship of God which was confessedly left unto them by Christ and his apostles. But the state of things is altered in the world. At a convention of the apostles and others, wherein the Holy Ghost did peculiarly preside, when the question about impositions was agitated, it was concluded that nothing should be imposed on the disciples but what was necessary for them to observe antecedently to any impositions, Acts xv. 28, 29; necessary, though not in their own nature, yet in the posture of things in the churches; necessary to the avoidance of scandal, whereby the observation of that injunction was to be regulated. Nor was there among the things called necessary the imposition of any one thing positively to be practised by any of the disciples in the worship of God, but only an abridgment of their liberty in some few external things, to which it did really extend. But that spirit of wisdom, moderation, and tenderness, whereby they were guided, being rejected by men, they began to think that they might multiply impositions as to the positive practice of the disciples of Christ in the worship of God at their pleasure, so that they could pretend that they were indifferent in themselves before the imposition of them; which gives, as they say, a necessity to their observation: which proceeding must be left to the judgment-seat of Jesus Christ, Matt. xxv. 45.

It is not worth our stay to consider what is pretended concerning the antiquity of liturgies, from some yet extant that bear the names of some of the apostles or evangelists. There is one that is called by the name of James, printed in Greek and Latin; another ascribed unto Peter, published by Lindanus; one also to Matthew, called the Ethiopic; another to Mark; which are in the Bible[1] P.P. And pains have been taken by Santesius, Pamelius, and others, to prove them genuine; but so much in vain as certainly nothing could be more. Nor doth Baronius in their Lives dare ascribe any such thing unto them. We need not any longer stay to remove this rubbish out of our way. They must be strangers to the spirit, doctrine, and writings of the apostles, who can impose such trash upon them as these liturgies are stuffed withal. The common use of words in them not known in the ages of the apostles, nor of some of them ensuing; the parts in them whose contrivers and framers are known to have lived many ages after; the mentioning of such things in them as were not once dreamed of in the days whereunto they pretend; the remembrance of them in them, as long before them deceased, who are suggested to be their authors; the preferring of other liturgies before them when once liturgies came in use, with a neglect of them; with the utter silence of the first Christian writers,

---

1 So the words are given in the original and subsequent editions. The reference is to the "Bibliotheca Patrum," in the second volume of which the liturgies mentioned will be found, —ED.

stories, councils, concerning them, do abundantly manifest that they are plainly suppositions of a very late fraud and invention. Yea, we have testimonies clear enough against this pretence in Gregor., lib. vii. epist. 63. Alcuinus, Amatorius, Rabanus, Lib. P. P. tom. x.; with whom consent Walafridus Strabo, Rupertus Titiensis, Berno, Radulphus Tangrensis, and generally all that have written any thing about liturgies in former days; many of whom show how, when, and by whom, the several parts of that public form which at length signally prevailed were invented and brought into use.

CHAPTER V.

The practice of the churches in the first three centuries as to forms of public worship — No set forms of liturgies used by them — The silence of the first writers concerning them — Some testimonies against them.

It is not about stinted forms of prayer in the worship and service of God, by those who, of their own accord, do make use of that kind of assistance, judging that course to be better than any thing they can do themselves in the discharge of the work of the ministry, but of the imposition of forms on others who desire "to stand fast in the liberty with which Christ hath made them free," that we inquire. This freedom we have manifested to have been purchased for them by the Lord Jesus, and the use of it continued by the apostles in their own practice, and to the churches planted by themselves; and this will one day appear to have been a sufficient plea for the maintenance of that liberty to the end of the world. Now, though what is purely matter of fact among the succeeding churches be not so far argumentative as to be insisted on as a rule exactly binding us to the imitation of it, yet it is deservedly worthy of great consideration, and not hastily to be rejected, unless it be discovered to have been diverse from the word, whereunto we are bound in all things to attend. We shall, therefore, make some inquiry into the practice of those churches, as to this matter of prescribing of forms of prayer in public church administrations, so far as any thing thereof is, by good antiquity, transmitted unto us.

Our first inquiry shall be into the three first centuries, wherein, confessedly, the streams of gospel institutions did run more clear and pure from human mixtures than in those following, although few of the teachers that were of note do escape from animadversions from those that have come after them. It cannot be denied but that for the most part the churches and their guides, within the space of the time limited, walked in the paths marked out for them by the apostles, and made conspicuous by the footsteps of the first churches planted by them. It doth not, then, appear, for aught as I can yet discover, that there was any attempt to invent, frame, and compose any liturgies or prescribed forms of administering the ordinances of the gospel, exclusive to the discharge of that duty by virtue of spiritual gifts received from Jesus Christ, much less for an imposition of any such forms on the consciences and practice of all the ministers of the churches within the time mentioned. If any be contrary-minded, it is incumbent on them to evince their assertion by some instances of unquestionable truth. As yet, that I know of, this is not performed by any. Baronius, ad an. Christi 58, num. 102–104, etc., treating expressly of the public prayers of the ancient Christians, is wholly silent as to the use of any forms amongst them, though he contends for their worshipping towards the east: which custom, when it was introduced, is most uncertain; but most certain that by many it was immoderately abused, who expressly worshipped the rising sun: of which abominable idolatry among Christians Leo complains, Serm. vii. De Nativitate. Indeed, the cardinal, ad an. 63, 12, 17, faintly contends that some things in the liturgy of James were composed by him, because some passages and expressions of it are used by Cyril of Jerusalem in his Mystagog. v.; but whereas Cyril lived not within the time limited unto our inquiry, and those treatises are justly suspected to be suppositions, nor is the testimony of that liturgy once cited or mentioned by him, the weakness of this insinuation is evident. Yea, it is most probable, that whosoever was the composer of that forged liturgy, he took those passages out of those reputed writings of Cyril, which were known in the church long before the name of the other was heard of. I know no ground of expectation of the performance of that which, as yet, men have come short in, — namely, in producing testimonies for the use of such liturgies as we are inquiring after; considering the diligence, ability, and interest of those who have been already engaged in that inquiry. Now, the silence of those who, in all probability, would have given an account of them had any such been in use in their days, with the description they give us of such a performance of the worship of God in the assemblies of Christians as is inconsistent with, and exclusive of, such prescribed forms as we treat of, is as full an evidence in this kind as our negative is capable of. In those golden fragments of antiquity which we have preserved by Eusebius, — I mean the Epistles of the church of Smyrna about the martyrdom of Polycarpus, and of the churches of Vienne and Lyons concerning their persecution, — we have not the least intimation of any such forms of service. In the Epistle of Clemens, or the church of Rome to the church of Corinth, in those of Ignatius, in the writings of Justin Martyr, Clemens, Tertullian, Origen, Cyprian, and their contemporaries, there is the same silence concerning them. The pseudographical writings that bear the names of the men of those days, with any pretence of considerable antiquity, as the Canons of the Apostles, Quæstiones ad Orthodoxos, Dionysius Hierarch. Divin. Nom., will not help in the cause; for though in some of them there are prayers mentioned, — and that for and about such things as were not "in rerum natura" in the days wherein those persons lived unto whose names they are falsely ascribed, — yet they speak nothing to the point of liturgies as stated in our inquiry. Something, I confess, may be found in some of the writings of some one or two of those of the third century, intimating the use of some particular prayers in some churches. So Origen, Homil. xi. in Hierimea: "Ubi frequenter in oratione dicimus, 'Da omipotens, da nobis partem cum prophetis, da cum apostolis Christi tui, tribue ut inveniamur ad vestigia unigeniti tui.'" But whether he speaks of a form or of the matter only of prayer, I know not. But such passages belong not unto our purpose. Those who deal expressly about the order, state, and condition of the churches, and the worship of God in them, their prayers and supplications, knew nothing of prescribed liturgies; yea, they affirm plainly that which is inconsistent with the use of them. The account given of the worship of the Christians in those days by Justin Martyr and Tertullian is known as having been often pleaded. I shall only mention it in our passage, and begin with the latter. "Illuc," saith he, (that is, towards heaven,) "suspicientes Christiani," (not like the idolaters, who looked their idols and images,) "manibus expansis," (not embracing altars or images, as did the heathen,) "quia innocuis, capite nudo, quia non erubescimus, denique sine monitore, quia de pectore oramus," (not as who repeat their prayers after their priests or sacrificers, but pouring out our prayers conceived in our breasts,) Apol., cap. xxx. And again, cap. xxxix.: "Corpus sumus de conscientia, religionis et disciplinæ unitate, et spei fœdere coimus in cætum et congregationem, ut ad Deum quasi vi facta precationibus ambiamus orantes. Hæc vis Deo grata est. Oramus etiam," etc. Whether this description of the public worship of the Christians in those days be consistent with the prescribed forms contended about, impartial men may easily discern.

The former treateth of the same matter in his Apology, in several places of it: Ἄθεοι μὲν οὖν ὡς οὐκ ἐσμέν, τὸν δημιουργὸν τῶν δὲ τοῦ παντὸς σεβόμενοι, ἀνενδεῆ αἱμάτων καὶ σπονδῶν καὶ θυμιάματων, ὡς ἐδιδάχθημεν λέγοντες, λόγῳ εὐχῆς καὶ εὐχαριστίας ἐφ' οἷς προσφερόμεθα πᾶσιν ὅση δύναμις αἰνουντες· — "Atheists," saith he, "we are not, seeing we worship the Maker of the world; affirming, indeed, as we are taught, that he stands in no need of blood, drink-offerings, or incense. In all our oblations we praise him according to our abilities, with" (or in the way of) "prayer and thanksgivings." This was, it seems, the liturgy of the church in the days of Justin Martyr; they called upon God with prayer and thanksgivings, according to the abilities they had received. The like account he gives of the prayers of persons converted, to prepare themselves for baptism; as also of the prayers of the administrators of that ordinance. Afterward, also, treating of the joining the baptized person unto the church, and the administration of the Lord's supper in the assembly, he adds: Μετὰ τὸ οὕτως λοῦσαι τὸν πεπεισμένον, καὶ συγκατατεθειμένον, ἐπὶ τοὺς λεγομένους ἀδελφοὺς ἄγομεν ἔνθα συνηγμένοι εἰσί, κοινὰς εὐχὰς ποιησόμενοι ὑπὲρ τὲ ἑαυτῶν, καὶ τοῦ φωτισθέντος, etc. — "After the believer who is joined unto us is thus washed, we bring him to those who are called brethren" (that is, the body of the church), "thither where they are gathered together for to make their prayers and supplications for themselves, and him who is" (newly) "illuminated," etc. These prayers, he declares afterward, were made by him who did preside among the brethren in the assembly, — that is, the bishop or pastor; who, when he had finished his prayer, the whole people cried, Amen; which leaves small room for the practice of any liturgy that is this day extant, or that hath left any memory of itself in this world. These prayers and supplications, he addeth, the president of the assembly ὅση δύναμις αὐτῷ ἀναπέμπει, "poureth out according to his ability;" and ἐπὶ πολὺ ποιεῖται, he "doth this work at large," or continues long in his work (of praises unto God in the name of Jesus Christ). I know some have excepted against the usual interpretation of these words, ὅση δύναμις, although they have not been able to assign any other tolerable sense unto them besides that which they would willingly oppose. But as the rendering of them "According to his ability," or, "As he is able," may not only be justified, but evinced to be the only sense the words are capable of, so the argument in hand doth not, as to its efficacy, depend on the precise signification of those two words, but on the whole contexture of the holy martyr's discourse; so relating to the worship of the churches in those days as to manifest that the use of prescribed forms of liturgies to be read in them was then utterly unknown.

I suppose it will be granted, that the time we have been inquiring into, — namely, the first three hundred years after Christ, — was the time of the church's greatest purity, though out of her greatest prosperity; that the union of the several churches was preserved beyond what afterward was ever in a gospel way attained, and the uniformity in worship which Christ requires observed amongst them; but all this while the use of these liturgies was utterly unknown: which makes the case most deplorable, that it should now be made the hinge whereon the whole exercise of the ministry must turn, it being a thing not only destitute of any warrant from Christ and his apostles, but utterly unknown to those churches whose antiquity gives them deservedly reverence with all; and so cannot claim its spring and original antecedent to such miscarryings and mistakes in the churches as all acknowledge to deserve a narrow and serious weighing and consideration. We may, then,

Chapter V.

I suppose, without giving occasion to the just imputation of any mistake, affirm, That the composing and imposition of liturgies, to be necessarily used or read in the administration of the ordinances of the gospel, is destitute of any plea or pretence, from Scripture or antiquity.

CHAPTER VI.

The pretended antiquity of liturgies disproved — The most ancient — Their variety — Canons of councils about forms of church administrations — The reasons pleaded in the justification of the first invention of liturgies answered — Their progress and end.

CONSIDERING with what confidence the antiquity of liturgies in the churches of Christ hath been pretended, it may seem strange to some that we should so much as attempt to divest them of that plea and pretence. But the love of the truth enforceth us to contend against many prejudices in this matter. May a denial of their antiquity, with the reasons of that denial tendered, provoke any to assert it by such testimonies as we have not as yet had the happiness to come to an acquaintance with, the advantage as well as the trouble will be theirs who shall so do. Only, in their endeavour to that purpose, I shall desire of them that they would not labour to impose on those whom they undertake to inform, by the ambiguous use of some word among the ancients; nor conclude a prescribed form of administration when they find mention of the administration itself; nor reckon reading of the Scriptures or singing of psalms as parts of the liturgy contended about; nor, from the use of some particular prayer by some persons, argue for the equity or necessity of composing such entire liturgies, or offices as they call them, for all evangelical administrators, and their necessary observation. So that these conditions be observed, I shall profess myself much engaged unto any one who shall discover a rise of them within the limits of the antiquity that hath been usually pretended and pleaded in their justification and practice. For my part, I know not any thing that ever obtained a practice and observation among Christians, whose springs are more dark and obscure than those of liturgies. They owe not their original to any councils, general or provincial; they were not the product of the advice or consent of any churches, nor was there any one of them at any time completed. No pleas can I as yet discover in them of old about uniformity in their use, or any consent in them about them. Every church seemeth to have done what seemed good in the church's own eyes, after once the way unto the use of them was opened. To whom in particular we are indebted for that invention, I know not; it may be those who are wiser do, and I wish they would value the thanks that they may have for the discovery when they shall be pleased to make it. They seem to me to have had but slender originals. One invented one form of prayer, or thanksgiving, or benediction; another added to what he had found out, — which was the easier task. Future additions gave some completeness to their beginners. Those in the Greek church, which bear the names of Chrysostom and Basil, seem to be the first that ever extended themselves to the whole worship of the church. Not that by them whose names they bear they were composed as now they appear, unless we shall think that they wrote them after their decease; but probably they collected some forms into order that had been by others invented, making such additions themselves as they judged needful, and so commended the use of them to the churches wherein they did preside. The use of them being arbitrarily introduced was not, by any injunction we find, made necessary; much less did any one single form plead for a general necessity. In the Latin church, Ambrose used one form, Gregory another, and Isidore a third. Nor is it unlikely but the liturgies were as many as the episcopal churches of those days. Hence, in the beginning of the fifth century, in an African council, can. 70, which is the 103d in the Codex Can. African., it is provided that no prayers be read in the administration of the eucharist but such as have been approved in some council, or have been observed by some prudent men formerly; which canon, with some addition, is confirmed in the second Milevitan council, can. 12: and the reason given in both is, lest there should any thing contrary to the faith creep into their way of worship. But this, as I said, was in the beginning of the fifth century, after divers forms of administration of holy things in the church had by divers been invented. The finding out of this invention was the act of some particular men, who have not been pleased to acquaint us with the reason of their undertaking. As yet it doth not appear unto us that those reasons could possibly be taken from the word, the practice of the apostles, or the churches by them planted, or those which followed them for some generations, nor from any council held before their days; and so, it may be, we are not much concerned to inquire what they were. Yet what is at present pleaded in the behalf of the first composers of liturgies may, in the way, be chiefly considered. Necessity is the first thing usually pretended. Many men being put into the office of the ministry who had not gifts and abilities for the profitable discharge of the work of the ministry, unto the edification of the church, they who had the oversight of them, according to the custom of those days, were enforced to compose such forms for their use as they judged expedient; so providing for the edification of the church, which else would have suffered from their weakness and insufficiency. Besides, many parts of the world, especially the east, in those days swarmed with antitrinitarian heretics of sundry sorts, who, many of them, by unsuspected wiles and dissimulations, and subscriptions of confessions, endeavoured to creep into the office of the ministry of the church, partly out of blind zeal to diffuse the poison of their abominations, partly out of carnal policy to be made partakers of the advantages which for the most part attended the orthodox profession. This increased the necessity of composing such forms of public worship as, being filled with expressions pointed against the errors of the times, might be a means to keep seducers from imposing themselves on ecclesiastical administrations. Thus there is no ancient liturgy, but it is full of the expressions that had been consented upon in the councils that were convened for the condemnation of those errors which were in their days most rife and pernicious. On this ground do learned men of all sorts conclude the liturgy falsely ascribed to James to be younger than the Nicene and Ephesine councils, from the use of the words ὁμοούσιος and θεότοκος in it.

But it doth not yet appear that these reasons were sufficient to justify such an innovation in the churches of Christ; for supposing that there were such a decay of gifts and abilities among them that were called to the administration of gospel institutions, that they were not able to discharge their duty in that work to the edification of the church, in like manner as those had done who went before them, this must needs have come to pass, either because our Lord Jesus Christ did cease to give out his gifts to his church, as he had done in former days upon his usual terms, or that men were negligent and careless in the receiving of them from him, — either not seeking them at his hand, or not exercising and improving of them according to his will and command. Other reason of this decay that I know of cannot be assigned. To affirm the former, on any pretence whatever, is blasphemously to accuse our Lord Jesus Christ of breach of promise, he having solemnly engaged to be with his disciples, not for an age or two, but to the end of the world, and that by the graces and gifts of his Spirit. I know it is pretended, that when Christians were multiplied there was a necessity of appointing them officers who had not the gifts and qualifications that otherwise would have been esteemed necessary; but I know withal that it is impossible Christians should be multiplied in the way of Christ faster than he is ready to give out gifts for their edification. The latter reason above, then, must be granted to be the cause of the defect of abilities in church officers, pleaded in the justification of the introduction into the church of composed forms of administration to be read by them. I wish, then, we might, in the fear of the Lord, consider whether the remedy were well suited unto the disease. I suppose all impartial men will grant that there ought to have been a return unto Him endeavoured from whom they were gone astray; at least gospel means used for the obtaining of those gifts of Christ, and the improving of them being received. Finding themselves at the loss wherein they were, should they not have searched their hearts and ways, to consider wherefore it was that the presence of Christ was so withdrawn from them, that they were so left without the assistance which others ministering in their places before them had received? Should not they have pulled out their single talent, and fallen to trading with it, that it might have increased under their care? Was not this the remedy and cure of the breach made by them, that God and man expected from them? Was it just, then, and according to the mind of Christ, that, instead of an humble returnal unto a holy, evangelical dependence on himself, they should invent an expedient to support them in the condition wherein they were, and so make all such returnal for hereafter needless? Yet this they did in the invention of liturgies, — they found out a way to justify themselves in their spiritual negligence and sloth, and to render a dependence on the Lord Christ for supplies of his Spirit, to enable them unto gospel administrations, altogether needless; they had now provided themselves with an ability they could keep in the church, so that he might keep the furniture of his Spirit unto himself. And this quickly became the most poisonous ingredient in the apostasy of the latter times.

Nor is there any sufficient warrant for this invention in the second pretence. There were many antichrists in the apostles' time, yet they never thought of this engine for their discovery or exclusion out of the church. Confessions of faith, or acknowledged forms of wholesome words, with the care of the disciples of Christ, or his churches, which are enabled by him to judge and discern of truth and error, are the preservations against the danger intimated that the gospel hath provided.

This being the entrance that the liturgies inquired after made into the churches of God, we are not much concerned to inquire what was their progress. That in the western parts of the world they all at length centred in the Roman mass-book and rituals we know. Their beginnings were small, plain, brief; their use arbitrary; the additions they received were from the endeavours of private men in several ages, occasional for the most part; the number of them great, equal to the various denominations of the churches; until the papal authority growing absolute and uncontrollable, the Roman form was imposed on the world, that, by innumerable artifices in a long tract of ages, was subjected thereunto, and that contrary to the determination of former Roman bishops, who advised the continuance of the different forms of administration which were in use in sever-

Chapter VI.

al churches: "Mihi placet, ut sive in Romanis sive in Galliarum partibus, seu in quÂlibet ecclesiÂ aliquid invenisti quod plus omnipotenti Deo possit placere sollicitè eligas," Greg. Resp. ad Interrogat. August. This being the state and condition, this the issue, that the invention of liturgies to be read in the worship of God was come unto before the Reformation, I shall briefly subjoin unto it an account of what was done in these kingdoms in reference unto it; which will make way to the clear stating of the question in particular that we are farther to speak unto. The history of our Reformation is known. I shall not speak any thing that may reflect with the least dishonour on the work or the workmen. We have abundant cause to bless the Lord continually for the one and the other. Yet still we must remember that our Reformers were men, and that the Reformation was a work performed by men. The former never claimed infallibility, nor the latter, that I know of, perfection; so that some things that were done by the one and in the other may admit of new considerations, without the reflection of any thing upon them that the one and the other would not readily and willingly admit. I shall therefore briefly give an account of that part of the work which concerns our business in hand. What was the state of this nation at the time of the Reformation, and what were the minds of the greater part of men in it in reference unto the work, is sufficiently declared in all the stories of those days. God having been pleased to send the saving light of the gospel into the minds and hearts of them in chief rule, — that is, King Edward and some of his counsellors, — they found no small difficulties to wrestle withal in dealing with the inveterate prejudices wherewith the generality of men were possessed against the work they intended. The far greater part of the clergy, true to their carnal present interest, with all their might and cunning opposed their endeavours. The greatest part of the nobility averse to their proceedings; the body of the people, blinded with superstition and profaneness, easily excited by the priests (whose peculiar concernment lay in keeping all things in their old channel and course) to make head against their proceedings; foreign nations round about fomenting to the uttermost all home-bred discontents, and offering themselves, by the instigation of the pope, to hinder the work by all ways that possibly they could imagine; — amongst all these the body of the people, which are the king's most special care, as they are his strength and wealth, were looked on as most to be regarded, as without whose concurrence their discontents of all others were likely only to consume themselves. Now, the people being in those days very ignorant, and unacquainted with the doctrines of the Scripture, were very little or not at all concerned what persuasion men were of in religion, as to the articles of pure belief, so as they might retain the "agenda" in the worship of God which they had been accustomed unto. Hence it was that those prelates, who were the instruments of the papal persecution in this nation, wisely stated the whole cause of their cruelty to be the Mass, or the worship of the church, seldom, unless compelled by disputations, once mentioning of the articles of faith, which yet they knew to be the main foundation of the difference between themselves and the reformers; because in this particular they had the advantage of the popular favour, the people violently interposing themselves in the behalf of that part of the present religion wherein their only share did lie. Had they laid the reasons and grounds of their quarrel in the differences of opinions about the "credenda" of the gospel, they would scarcely have prevailed with the common people to carry fagot for the burning of their brethren for things whereof they understood little or nothing at all.

Our wise and provident reformers, considering this state of things and temper of the minds of men, however they resolvedly declared for the "credenda" of the gospel, and asserted the articles of faith from which the Roman church had most eminently apostatized, yet found it their concernment to attemper the way of public worship, as much as possible with consistency with the articles of the faith they professed, to that which the popularity had been inured unto. Observing plainly that all their concernment in religion lay in the outward worship whereunto they had been accustomed, having very confused apprehensions of the speculative part of it, it was easy for them to apprehend that if they could condescend to furnish them with such a way thereof as might comply in some reasonable manner with their former usage, these two things would ensue:— First, That the main reformation, in the doctrine, which alone would deliver the people from their prejudicate opinions about the worship of God, would be carried on with less noise and observation, and consequently less contest and opposition; for whilst they had a way and form of worship proposed to them wherewith they could be contented, those that were wiser might believe and teach what they pleased: which, in the providence of God, proved in a short time a blessed means of delivering them from their old entanglements and darkness. Secondly, That their priests, who were the chief instigators to all disorder and opposition to the whole work of reformation, finding a way proposed for their continuance in the possession of their places, and a worship prescribed which they could as easily perform and go through withal as what they had practised in former days, might possibly acquiesce in the proceedings of their betters, finding the temporal interest, which they chiefly respected, to be saved. And this afterward, accordingly, they did, reading the service-book instead of the mass; without which supply of such wants and defects in them as I shall not name, they would never have entertained any thoughts of owning the Reformation, nor of suffering the people to submit themselves thereunto. On these considerations, and for these ends, it is evident, from the story of those times, that our present liturgy was framed. Rejecting out of the offices before in use such things as were directly contrary to the articles of faith protested in the reformation in hand, translating of what remained into English, with such supplies and alterations as the rejection of those things before mentioned made necessary, the book mentioned, in some haste, and with some other disadvantages for such a work, was by our first reformers compiled. And, indeed, somewhat there was in this case not much unlike that insisted on in the entrance of this discourse between the believing Jews and Gentiles. Many of the Jews who were willing to receive Christ's reformation in point of faith and obedience, yet pertinaciously adhered to their old ceremonious worship, violently setting themselves against any that durst speak a word against its continuance. That there might not be an endless contest and strife about the matter, and so the progress of the gospel be hindered amongst the one sort and the other, the apostles taking in hand the old worship, as to the Gentile worshippers, whose case above came then under consideration, they reject and declare abrogate all such ceremonies whose necessary observation had an inconsistency with the doctrine of the gospel, proposing only some few things to be observed, which occasioned the greatest difference between the parties at variance.

Now, as this composition of that difference was accommodated to the present scandal, and the obligation unto its observation to be regulated thereby; so by the removal thereof, itself, as unto any use in the church of Christ, did expire. Not unlike unto this of the apostles seems the aim of our first reformers to have been; that they might win the people, who had been accustomed to the way of worship in use in the Papacy, unto a compliance with the doctrine of the gospel, and that there might not be endless contests about that which was presently to be practised, — which perhaps they thought of small importance in comparison of those weighty fundamental truths which they had endeavoured to acquaint them with, and bring them to the belief of, — they provided for the use of such parts of it and in such a manner as were not openly inconsistent with the truths which was in their hearts to communicate unto them. And it is not impossible but that this constitution might have had the same end with the other, if not of present use, being of things of another nature, yet of a timely expiration, when notoriously useless as to the main ends intended in it, had not the interest of some interposed for its continuance beyond the life and influence of all or any of those causes or occasions. And hence it is that those streams at this day run strongly and fiercely, by the addition and pouring into of adventitious rivulets, with showers or rather storms of temporal interest, whose springs are all utterly long since dried up.

The Book of Common Prayer being composed as hath been declared, became from its very cradle and infancy a bone of contention to the church of God in this nation. Many of the people and ministers, who seemed to be enlightened with a beam of truth of an equal lustre and brightness with that which

Chapter VI.

shined in the minds of their brethren, wholly decried that prudential compliance with the people's ignorance and adherence to Popery, which was openly avowed in the composition and imposition of it, and called earnestly for a purer way of the administration of gospel ordinances, more agreeable to the word and primitive times, than they apprehended that prescribed form to contain and exhibit. Others, again, in the justification of that whereof themselves were the authors, laboured to recommend the book, not only as to truth, but as useful and very beneficial for the edification of the church. It is known, also, that the contests of men in this nation about this form of divine service were not confined to this nation, but were carried by them into other parts of the world. And should I pursue the suffrage that hath lain against it, from the first day of its composure to this wherein we live, never giving it a quiet possession in the minds and consciences of men, with the various evils that have all along attended its imposition, I suppose it might of itself prevail with sober men, who desire their moderation should be known to all, because the Judge standeth at the door, to take the whole matter of the imposition of this or the like form once more under a sedate consideration. And they may, perhaps, be the rather induced thereunto, if they will but impartially weigh that the opposition to the imposed liturgy hath increased daily, according to the increase of light and gospel gifts among men: so that there seems to be no way to secure its station but by an opposition unto them and extirpation of them; which is a sad work for any that are called Christians to engage into.

I presume the conscientious reader will be able to discover, from what hath been spoken, rules sufficient to guide his judgment in reference unto the use of prescribed liturgies. The story of their rise and progress is enough to plead for a liberty from an indispensable necessity of their observation. That which is of pure human invention, and comparatively of late and uncertain original, whose progress hath been attended with much superstition and persecution, stands in need of very cogent reasons to plead for its continuance; for others will not outbalance the evils that are asserted to flow from it. But it may be this will not suffice with some for a final decision and determination of this difference. I shall, therefore, briefly state the question about them, which only I shall speak unto, and try their use and usefulness by that infallible rule by which both we and they must be judged another day.

CHAPTER VII.

The question stated — First argument against the composing and imposing of liturgies — Arbitrary additions to the worship of God rejected — Liturgies not appointed by God — Made necessary in their imposition, and a part of the worship of God — Of circumstances of worship — Instituted adjuncts of worship not circumstances — Circumstances of actions, as such, not circumstances of worship — Circumstances commanded made parts of worship — Prohibitions of additions produced, considered, applied.

To clear up what it is in particular that we insist upon, some few things are to be premised:— First, then, I do not in especial intend the liturgy now in use in England, any farther than to make it an instance of such imposed liturgies, whereof we treat. I shall not, then, at all inquire what footing it hath in the law, how nor when established, nor what particular failings are pleaded to be in it, nor what conformity it bears with the Roman offices, with the like things that are usually objected against it. Nor, secondly, do I oppose the directive part of this liturgy as to the reading of the Scripture, when it requires that which is Scripture to be read, the administration of the ordinances by Christ appointed, nor the composition of forms of prayer suited to the nature of the institutions to which they relate, so they be not imposed on the administrators of them to be read precisely as prescribed. But, thirdly, this is that alone which I shall speak unto, — the composing of forms of prayer in the worship of God, in all gospel administrations, to be used by the ministers of the churches, in all public assemblies, by a precise reading of the words prescribed unto them, with commands for the reading of other things, which they are not to omit, upon the penalty contained in the sanction of the whole service and the several parts of it. The liberty which some say is granted for a man to use his own gifts and abilities in prayer before and after sermons, will, I fear, as things now stand, upon due consideration, appear rather to be taken than given. However, it concerns not our present question, because it is taken for granted by those that plead for the strict observation of a book, that the whole gospel worship of God, in the assemblies of Christians, may be carried on and performed without any such preaching as is prefaced with the liberty pretended.

These things being premised, I shall subjoin some of the reasons that evidently declare the imposition and use of such a liturgy or form of public words to be contrary to the rule of the word, and consequently sinful.

First, the arbitrary invention of any thing, with commands for its necessary and indispensable use in the public worship of God, as a part of that worship, and the use of any thing so invented and so commanded in that worship, is unlawful, and contrary to the rule of the word; but of this nature is the liturgy we treat of. It is an invention of men, not appointed, not commanded of God; it is commanded to be used in the public worship of God, by reading the several parts of it, according to the occasions that they respect, and that indispensably; and is made a part of that worship.

There are three things affirmed in the assumption concerning the liturgy:— *First*, That it is not appointed or commanded of God; that is, there is no command of God either for the use of this or that liturgy in particular, nor in general that any such should so be, and be so used as is pleaded. And this we must take for granted, until some instance of such command be produced. *Secondly*, That it is made necessary, by virtue of the commands of men, to be used in the public worship of God. About this there will be no difference. Let it be denied, and there is an end of all this strife. I shall not dispute about other men's practice. They who are willing to take it upon their consciences that the best way to serve God in the church, or the best ability that they have for the discharge of their duty therein, consists in the reading of such a book (for I suppose they will grant that they ought to serve God with the best they have), shall not by me be opposed in their way and practice. It is only about

Chapter VII.

its imposition, and the necessity of its observance by virtue of that imposition, that we discourse. Now, the present command is, that such a liturgy be always used in the public worship of God, and that without the use or reading of it the ordinances of the gospel be not administered at any time, nor in any place, with strong pleas for the obligation arising from that command, making the omission of its observance to be sinful. It is, then, utterly impossible that any thing should be more indispensably necessary than the reading of the liturgy in the worship of God is. It is said, indeed, that it is not commanded as though in itself it were necessary, either a prescribed liturgy, or this or that, for then it were sin in any not to use it, whether it were commanded by the church or not; but for order, uniformity, conveniency, and the preventing of sundry evils that would otherwise ensue, it is commanded: which command makes the observation of it necessary unto us. But we are not as yet inquiring what are the reasons of its imposition; they may afterward be spoken unto. And time also may be taken to show that it were much more tolerable if men would plead for the necessity of the things which it seems good unto them to command, and on that ground to command their observance, than, granting them not necessary in themselves, to make them necessary to be observed merely by virtue of their commands, for reasons which they say satisfy themselves, but come short of giving satisfaction to them from whom obedience is required; for whereas the will of man can be no way influenced unto obedience but by mere acknowledged sovereignty, or conviction of reason in and from the things themselves, commands in and about things wherein they own not that the commanders have an absolute sovereignty (as God hath in all things, the civil supreme magistrate in things civil that are good and lawful), nor can they find the reasons of the things themselves cogent, are a yoke which God hath not designed the sons of men to bear. But it is concerning the necessary use of the liturgy in the worship of God that we are disputing; which, I suppose, will not be denied.

[Thirdly,] It remaineth, then, to consider whether the use of the liturgy as prescribed be made a part of the worship of God. Now, that wherewith and whereby God is commanded to be worshipped, and without which all observation or performance of his public worship is forbidden, is itself made a part of his worship. The command, "With this (or thus) shall you worship God," makes the observation of that command a part of God's worship. It is said that it is only a circumstance of worship, but no part of it. Prayer is the worship of God; but that *this prayer* shall be used and no other is only a circumstance of it: so that though it may be possibly accounted a circumstance or accidentary part of God's worship, yet it is not asserted to be of the substance of it. How far this is so, and how far it is otherwise must be considered. Circumstances are either such as follow actions as actions, or such as are arbitrarily superadded and adjoined by command unto actions, which do not of their own accord, nor naturally nor necessarily attend them. Now, religious actions in the worship of God are actions still. Their religious relation doth not destroy their natural being. Those circumstances, then, which do attend such actions as actions not determined by divine institution, may be ordered, disposed of, and regulated by the prudence of men. For instance, prayer is a part of God's worship. Public prayer is so, as appointed by him. This, as it is an action to be performed by man, cannot be done without the assignment of time, and place, and sundry other things, if order and conveniency be attended to. These are circumstances that attend all actions of that nature, to be performed by a community, whether they relate to the worship of God or no. These men may, according as they see good, regulate and change as there is occasion; I mean, they may do so who are acknowledged to have power in such things. As the action cannot be without them, so their regulation is arbitrary, if they come not under some divine disposition and order, as that of time in general doth. There are also some things, which some men call circumstances, also, that no way belong of themselves to the actions whereof they are said to be the circumstances, nor do attend them, but are imposed on them, or annexed unto them, by the arbitrary authority of those who take upon them to give order and rules in such cases; such as to pray before an image or towards the east, or to use this or that form of prayer in such gospel administrations, and no other. These are not circumstances attending the nature of the thing itself, but are arbitrarily superadded to the things that they are appointed to accompany. Whatever men may call such additions, they are no less parts of the whole wherein they serve than the things themselves whereunto they are adjoined. The schoolmen tell us that that which is made so the condition of an action, that without it the action is not to be done, is not a circumstance of it, but such an adjunct as is a necessary part. But not to contend about the word, such additionals, that are called circumstantial, are made parts of worship as are made necessary by virtue of command to be observed. Sacrifices of old were the instituted worship of God. That they should be offered at the tabernacle or temple at Jerusalem, and nowhere else, was a circumstance appointed to be observed in their offerings; and yet this circumstance was no less a part of God's worship than the sacrifice itself. In the judgment of most men, not only prayer, and the matter of our prayer, is appointed by our Saviour in the Lord's prayer, but we are commanded also to use the very words of it. I desire to know whether the precise use of these words be not a part of God's worship? It seems that it is; for that which is commanded by Christ to be used in the worship of God is a part of God's worship. The case is the same here. Prayer is commanded, and the use of these prayers is commanded; the latter distinctly, as such, as well as the former, is made a part of God's worship. Nor is there any ground for that distinction of the circumstantial or accidentary part of God's worship, and worship substantially taken, or the substantial parts of it. The worship of God is either moral or instituted. The latter contains the peculiar ways and manner of exerting the former according to God's appointment. The actions whereby these are jointly discharged, or the inward moral principles of worship are exerted in and according to the outward institutions, have their circumstances attending them. These in themselves, nakedly considered, have in them neither good nor evil, nor are any circumstances in the worship of God, much less circumstantial parts of his worship, but only circumstances of those actions as actions whereby it is performed. And whatever is instituted of God in and about those circumstances is a substantial part of his worship.

Nor is the prescribing of such a form of prayer a regulation of those circumstances of public prayer, for decency, order, and uniformity, which attend it as a public action, but the superaddition of an adjunct condition, with which it is to be performed, and without which it is not to be performed as it is prayer, the worship of God. Of this nature was sacrificing of old on the altar at the tabernacle or temple, and there alone; and many more instances of the like nature may be given. Praising of God and blessing of the people were parts of the worship of God, appointed by himself to be performed by the priests under the law. In the doing thereof at certain seasons, they were commanded to use some forms of words prescribed unto them for that purpose. Not only hereby the praising and blessing of God, but the use of those forms in so doing, became a necessary part of the worship of God; and so was the use of organs and the like instruments of music, which respect that manner of praising him which God then required. The case is here no otherwise. Prayers and thanksgivings, in the administration of the ordinances of the gospel, are of the instituted worship of God. Unto these, as to the manner of their performance, is the imposition of the liturgical forms spoken of superadded, and their use made a necessary adjunct of the duty itself, so as that it may not be performed without them; which makes them a no less necessary part of the worship of God than any of his institutions of old were which related to the circumstances and the manner of his worship, as the temple, tabernacle, altar, forms of thanksgiving and confession, composed and prescribed by the Holy Ghost himself.

But I suppose this will not be much gainsaid; by some it is acknowledged in express terms. And for the matter of fact, we find that the reading of a book of service is with many taken not to be a part, but the whole of the worship of God, which if it be done, they suppose God is acceptably worshipped without more ado; and if it be omitted, whatever else be done in the room of it, that God is not worshipped at all.

Our inquiry, then, must be, whether such additions to or in the worship of God, besides or beyond his own institution and appointment, be allowable, or lawful to be practised. I shall first

CHAPTER VII. 51

recite the words in general of some testimonies that lie against such a practice, and then consider what they most particularly speak unto. Of this sort are Exod. xx. 4, 5: "Thou shalt not make unto thee any graven image, or any likeness of any thing that is in heaven above, or that is in the earth beneath, or that is in the water under the earth; thou shalt not bow down thyself to them, nor serve them: for I the LORD thy God am a jealous God, visiting the iniquity of the fathers upon the children," etc. Deut. iv. 2: "Ye shall not add unto the word which I command you, neither shall ye diminish ought from it, that ye may keep the commandments of the LORD your God which I command you." Chap. xii. 32: "What thing soever I command you, observe to do it: thou shalt not add thereto, nor diminish from it." Prov. xxx. 6: "Add not unto his words, lest he reprove thee, and thou be found a liar." Jer. vii. 31: "They have built the high places of Tophet, which is in the valley of the son of Hinnom, to burn their sons and their daughters in the fire; which I commanded them not, neither came it into my heart." Matt. xv. 9: "In vain do they worship me, teaching for doctrines the commandments of men." Ver. 13: "Every plant which my heavenly Father hath not planted, shall be rooted up." Also, Mark vii. 7, 8; Rev. xxii. 18: "If any man shall add unto these things, God shall add unto him the plagues that are written in this book." The mind of God in these and the like prohibitions, the reader may find exemplified, Lev. x. 1–3, etc.; Josh. xxii. 10, etc.; Judges viii. 24, etc.; 2 Kings xvi. 11, 12; 1 Chron. xv. 13, and in other places.

Men who, having great abilities of learning, are able to distinguish themselves from under the power of the most express rules and commands, should yet, methinks, out of a sense of their weakness (which they are ready to profess themselves convinced of when occasion is offered to deliver their thoughts concerning them), have compassion for those who, being not able to discern the strength of their reasonings, because of their fineness, are kept in a conscientious subjection to the express commands of God, especially conceiving them not without some cogent cause reiterated.

But lest the present exasperation of the spirits of men should frustrate that hope and expectation, let us consider what is the precise intendment of the testimonies produced, seeing we have reason to look well to the justice of our cause in the first place; which being cleared, we may the better be satisfied in coming short of favour where it may not be obtained. The places of Scripture produced are taken partly out of the Old Testament, partly out of the New. And I suppose it will be granted that there is an equal force of rule in the one as in the other; for though these in the Old Testament had their peculiar respect to the worship that was then instituted, yet they had [respect to it] not as then instituted, but as the worship which God himself had appointed. And therefore their general force abides while God requires any worship at the hands of men, unless it may be made appear that God hath parted with that prerogative of being the appointer of his own worship now under the New Testament, which he so vindicated unto himself under the Old. Take them, then, in their general aim and intention, that which these and the like testimonies unanimously speak unto us is this, That the will of God is the sole rule of his worship, and all the concernment of it, and that his authority is the sole principle and cause of the relation of any thing to his worship in a religious manner; and consequently, that he never did, nor ever will, allow that the wills of his creatures should be the rule or measure of his honour or worship, nor that their authority should cause any thing to hold a new relation unto him, or any other but what it hath by the law of its creation. And this is the sum and substance of the second commandment, wherein so great a cloud of expositors do centre their thoughts, that it will not be easy for any to withstand them; so that the other texts produced are express to all the particulars of the assertion laid down may be easily evinced.

    That the Lord asserts his own authority and will as the constituting cause and rule of all his worship was the first thing asserted. His repetition of "My words," "What I have commanded," and the like expressions, secure this enclosure. Unless men can pretend that there is the same reason of the words and commands of God himself, it is in vain for them to pretend a power of instituting any thing in the worship of God; for the formal reason of every such institution is, that the word of it is

Chapter VII.

the word of God. It is enough to discard any thing from a relation to the worship of God, to manifest that the appointers of it were men, and not God. Nor can any man prove that God hath delegated unto them his power in this matter; nor did he ever do so to any of the sons of men, — namely, that they should have authority to appoint any thing in his worship, or about it, that seemeth meet unto their wisdom. With some, indeed, in former days, he intrusted the work of revealing unto his church and people what he himself would have observed; which dispensation he closed in the person of Christ and his apostles. But to intrust men with authority, not to declare what he revealed, but to appoint what seemeth good unto them, he never did it; the testimonies produced lie evidently against it. Now, surely, God's asserting his own will and authority as the only rule and cause of his worship, should make men cautious how they suppose themselves like or equal unto him herein, especially being destitute of warrant from the approved example or precedent of any that have gone before them. If the example of any one in the Old or New Testament could be produced, that of his own mind and authority made any such additions to the worship of God as that which we treat about, by virtue of any trust or power pretended from or under him, and found acceptance in his so doing, or that was not severely rebuked for his sin therein, some countenance would seem to be given unto those that at present walk in such paths; although I suppose it would not be easy for thereto prove any particular instances, which might have peculiar exemption from the general law, which we know not, to be a sufficient warrant for their proceedings. But whereas God himself having instituted his own worship and all the concernments of it, doth also assert his own authority and will as the sole cause and rule of all the worship that he will accept, no instance being left on record of any one that ever made any additions to what he had appointed, on any pretence whatever, or by virtue of any authority whatever, that was accepted with him; and whereas the most eminent of those who have assumed that power to themselves, as also of the judgment of the reasons necessary for the exerting of it, as to matter and manner, have been given up, in the righteous judgment of God, to do things not convenient, yea, abominable unto him (as in the papal church), — it is not unlikely to be the wisdom of men to be very cautious of intruding themselves into this thankless office.

But such is the corrupt nature of man, that there is scarce any thing whereabout men have been more apt to contend with God from the foundation of the world. That their will and wisdom may have a share (some at least) in the ordering of his worship, is that which of all things they seem to desire. Wherefore, to obviate their pride and folly, to his asserting of his own prerogative in this matter, he subjoins severe interdictions against all or any man's interposing therein, so as to take away any thing by him commanded, or to add any thing to what is by him appointed. This also the testimonies recited fully express. The prohibition is plain, "Thou shalt not add to what I have commanded." Add not to his words, "That is, in his worship, to the things which by his word he hath appointed to be observed, — neither to the word of his institution nor to the things instituted." Indeed, adding things adds to the word; for the word that adds is made of a like authority with his. All *making to ourselves* is forbidden, though what we so make may seem unto us to tend to the furtherance of the worship of God. It is said men may add nothing to the substance of the worship of God, but they may order, dispose, and appoint the things that belong to the manner and circumstances of it, and this is all that is done in the prescription of liturgies. Of circumstances in and about the worship of God we have spoken before, and removed that pretence. Nor is it safe distinguishing in the things of God where himself hath not distinguished. When he gave out the prohibitions mentioned under the Old Testament, he was appointing or had appointed his whole worship, and all that belonged unto it, in matter and manner, way and order, substance and circumstance. Indeed, there is nothing in its whole nature, as it belongs to the general being of things, so circumstantial, but that if it be appointed by God in his worship, it becomes a part of the substance of it; nor can any thing that is not so appointed ever by any be made a circumstance of his worship, though many things are circumstances of those actions which in his worship are performed. This distinction, then, directly makes void the command, so that conscience cannot acquiesce in it. Besides, we have showed that liturgies prescribed and imposed are necessary parts of God's worship, and so not to be salved by this distinction.

Moreover, to testify what weight he laid on the observance of these general prohibitions, when men found out other ways of worship than what he had appointed, though the particulars were such as fell under other special interdictions, yet the Lord was pleased to place the great aggravation of their sin in the contempt of those general rules mentioned. This is that he urgeth them with, that they did things by him *not appointed*; of not observing any thing in religion but what he requires, that he presseth them withal. The command is general, "You shall add nothing to what I have instituted." And the aggravation of the sin pressed by him relates not to the particular nature of it, but to this general command or prohibition, "You have done what I commanded you not." That the particular evil condemned was also against other special commands of God, is merely accidental to the general nature of the crime they were urged withal. And whereas God hath given out these rules and precepts, "You shall do whatever I command you, and according as I command you; you shall add nothing thereunto, nor take any thing therefrom," can the transgression of this rule be any otherwise expressed but thus, "They did the thing which he commanded not nor did it ever come into his heart?"

It is said, that the intention of these rules and prohibitions is only to prevent the addition of what is contrary to what God hath appointed, and not of that which may tend to the furtherance and better discharge of his appointments. The usual answer to this acceptation is, that whatever is added is contrary to what is commanded, though not in this or that particular command, yet to that command that nothing be added. It is not the nature of any particular that is condemned, but the power of adding, in those prohibitions. Let us see, then, whether of these senses has the fairest evidence with the evident purport and intention of the rules, precepts, and prohibitions under consideration.

Our Lord Jesus Christ directs his apostles to teach his disciples "to do and observe whatever he commanded them." Those who contend for the latter interpretation of those and the like precepts before mentioned, affirm that there is in these words a restriction of the matter of their commission to the express commands of Christ. What he commands, they say, they were to teach men to observe, and nothing else; nor will he require the observance of aught else at our hands. The others would have his intention to be, whatever he commanded, and whatever seemeth good to them to command, so it be not contrary unto what was by him commanded; as if he had said, "Teach men to observe whatever I command them; and command you them to observe whatever you think meet, so it be not contrary to my commands." Certainly this gloss at first view seems to defeat the main intendment of Christ, in that express limitation of their commission unto his own commands. So also under the Old Testament: giving order about his worship, the Lord lets Moses know that he must do all things according to what he should show and reveal unto him. In the close of the work committed unto him, to show what he had done was acceptable to God, it is eight or ten times repeated that he did all as the Lord commanded him; nothing was omitted, nothing added by him. That the same course might be observed in the following practice which was taken in the first institution, the Lord commands that nothing be added to what was so appointed by him, nothing diminished from it. The whole duty, then, of the church, as unto the worship of God, seems to lie in the precise observation of what is appointed and commanded by him. To assert things may be added to the worship of God not by him appointed, which, in the judgment of those that add them, seem useful for the better performance of what he hath appointed, so that they be not contrary unto them, seems to defeat the whole end and intention of God in all those rules and prohibitions, if either the occasion, rise, cause of them, or their commendable observance, be considered. On these and no better terms is that prescribed liturgy we treat of introduced and imposed. It comes from man, with authority to be added to the worship that Christ requires, and ventures on all the severe interdictions of such additions, armed only with the pretence of not being contrary to any particular command in the matter of it (which yet is denied), and such distinctions as have not the least ground in Scripture, or in the reason of the things themselves which it is applied unto. Might we divert into particulars, it were easy to demonstrate that the instances given in the Scripture of God's rejection of such additions do abundantly obviate all the pleas that are insisted on for the waiving of the general prohibition.

CHAPTER VIII.

Of the authority needful for the constituting and ordering of any thing that is to have relation to God and his worship — Of the power and authority of civil magistrates — The power imposing the liturgy — The formal reason of religious obedience — Use of the liturgy an act of civil, not religious obedience, Matt. xxviii. 20 — No rule to judge of what is meet in the worship of God, but his word.

BESIDES the regulation of all our proceedings and actions in the worship of God by the command and prohibitions insisted on in the foregoing chapter, there are two things indispensably necessary to render the prescription of any thing in religious worship allowable or lawful to be observed, both pointed unto by the testimonies produced; and these are, — first, An *authority* to enjoin; and, secondly, A certain *rule* to try the injunction by.

The worship of God is of that nature that whatsoever is performed in it is an act of religious obedience. That any thing may be esteemed such, it is necessary that the conscience be in it subject to the immediate authority of God. His authority alone renders any act of obedience religious. All authority is originally in God, and there are two ways whereby he is pleased to exert it:— First, By a delegation of authority unto some persons for some ends and purposes; which they being invested withal, may command in their own names an observance of the things about which, by God's appointment, their authority is to be exercised. Thus is it with kings and rulers of the earth. They are powers ordained of God, having authority given them by him. And being invested with power, they give out their commands for the doing or performing of such or such things whereunto their authority doth extend. That they ought to be obeyed in things good and lawful, doth not arise from the authority vested in themselves, but from the immediate command of God that in such things they ought to be obeyed. Hence obedience in general unto magistrates is a part of our moral and religious obedience unto God, as it respects his command, whatever the nature and object of it be. But the performance of particular actions, wherein by their determination our obedience exerts itself, being resolved into that authority which is vested in them, is not religious but civil obedience, any otherwise than as in respect of its general nature it relates to the command of God in general. No act, I say, that we perform, whereof this is the formal reason, that it is appointed and commanded by man, though that man be intrusted with power from God to appoint and require acts of that nature, is an act of religious obedience unto God in itself, because it relates not immediately to his divine authority requiring that act.

Secondly, God doth exert his authority immediately, and that either directly from heaven, as in the giving of the law, or by the inspiration of others to declare his will; unto both which his word written answereth. Now, whatever is done in obedience to the authority of God thus exerting itself is a part of that religious duty which we owe to God, whether it be in his first institution and appointment, or any duty in its primitive revelation, or whether it be in the commands he gives for the observation of what he hath formerly appointed; for when God hath commanded any things to be observed in his worship, though he design and appoint men to see them observed accordingly, and furnish them with the authority of commanding to that purpose, yet the interposition of that authority of men, though by God's institution, doth not at all hinder but that the duty performed is religious obedience, relating directly to the will and command of God. The power commanding in the case we have in hand is man's, not that of the Lord; for though it be acknowledged that those who do command have their authority from God, yet unless the thing commanded be also in particular appointed by God, the obedience that is yielded is purely civil, and not religious. This is the state of the matter under consideration: The commanding and imposing power is variously apprehended. Some say it is the church that doth it, and so assert the authority to be ecclesiastical. "Every church," say they, "hath power to order things of this nature for order and decency's sake." When it is inquired what the church is that they intend, then some are at a loss, and would fain insinuate somewhat into our thoughts that they dare not openly assert and maintain. The truth is, the church in this sense is the king, or the king and parliament, by whose advice he exerts his legislative power. By their authority was the liturgy composed, or it was composed without authority; by their authority it must be imposed, if it be imposed. What is or was done in the preparation of it by others, unto their judgment, hath no more influence into the authoritative imposition of it than the act of a person learned in the law, drawing up a bill for the consideration of parliament, hath into its binding law-power when confirmed. In this sense we acknowledge the power ordaining and imposing this liturgy to be of God, to be good and lawful, to be obeyed unto the utmost extent of that obedience which to man can be due, and that upon the account of the institution and command of God himself; but yet, supposing the liturgy to fall within the precincts and limits of that obedience, the observance and use of it, being not commanded of God, is purely an act of civil obedience, and not religious, wherein the conscience lies in no immediate subjection to Jesus Christ. It is of the same general nature with the honest discharge of the office of a constable; and this seems inconsistent with the nature of the worship of God.

But whatever be the immediate imposing power, we have direction as to our duty in the last injunction of our blessed Saviour to his apostles, Matt. xxviii. 20, "Teaching them to observe all things whatsoever I have commanded." In things which concern the worship of God, the commanding power is Christ, and his command the adequate rule and measure of our obedience. The teaching, commanding, and enjoining of others to do and observe those commands, is the duty of those intrusted with Christ's authority under him. Their commission to teach and enjoin, and our duty to do and observe, have the same rules, the same measure, bounds, and limits. What they teach and enjoin beyond what Christ hath commanded, they do it not by virtue of any commission from him; what we do beyond what he hath commanded, we do it not in obedience to him; — what they so teach, they do it in their own name, not his; what we so do, we do in our own strength, not his, nor to his glory. The answer of Bellarmine to that argument of the protestant divines from this place, against the impositions of his church, is the most weak and frivolous that I think ever any learned man was forced to make use of; and yet where to find better will not easily occur. Our Lord Jesus Christ saith, "Go and teach men to observe whatsoever I have commanded you; and, lo, I am with you alway;" to which he subjoins, "It is true, but yet we are bound also to obey them that are set over us, — that is, our church guides;" and so leaves the argument as sufficiently discharged! Now, the whole question is concerning what those church guides may teach and enjoin, whereunto we are to give obedience, which is here expressly restrained to the things commanded by Christ; to which the cardinal offers not one word. The things our Saviour treats about are principally the "agenda" of the gospel, — things to be done and observed in the worship of God. Of these, as was said, he makes his own command the adequate rule and measure: "Teach men to observe" πάντα ὅσα "all whatsoever I command." In their so doing alone doth he promise his presence with them; that is, to enable them unto the discharge of their duty. He commands, I say, all that shall to the end of the world be called to serve him in the work of the gospel, to "teach." In that expression he compriseth their whole duty, as their whole authority is given them in this commission. In their teaching, indeed, they are to command with all authority; and upon the non-obedience of men unto their teaching, either by not receiving their word, or by walking unworthy of it when it is received in the profession of it, he hath allotted them the course of their whole proceedings; but still requiring that all be regulated by what they are originally commissionated and enabled to teach and command. Let, then, the imposition of a liturgy be tried by this rule. It was never by Christ commanded to his apostles, cannot by any be taught as his command; and therefore men, in the teaching or imposing of it, have no promise of his presence, nor do they that observe it yield any obedience unto him therein. This, I am sure, will be the rule of Christ's inquiry at his great visitation at the last day, — the things which himself hath commanded will be inquired after, as to some men's teachings, and all men's observation, and those only. And I cannot but admire with what peace and satisfaction to their own souls men can pretend to act as by commission from Christ, as the chief administrators of his gospel and worship on the earth, and make it their whole business almost to teach men to do and observe what he never commanded, and rigorously to inquire after and into the observation of their own commands, whilst those of the Lord Jesus are openly neglected.

But let the authority of men for imposition be supposed to equal the fancy of any who through ignorance or interest are most devoted unto it, when they come to put their authority into execution, commanding things in and about the worship of God, I desire to know by what rule they are to proceed in their so doing. All the actions of men are or ought to be regular: good or evil they are, as they answer to or dissent from their proper rule. The rule in this matter must be the word of God, or their own prudence. Allow the former to be the rule, — that is, revealing what they ought to command, — and there is a total end of this difference. What a rule the latter is like to prove is easy to conjecture; but there is no need of conjectures where experience interposeth. The great philosopher is blamed by some for inserting the determination of men wise and prudent into his definition of the rule of moral virtue; for they say, "That cannot be certainly known whose rule and measure is fluctuating and uncertain." If there be ground for this assertion in reference to moral virtues, whose seed and principles are inlaid in the nature of man, how much more is that rule to be questioned when applied to things whose spring and foundation lies merely in supernatural revelation? How various, uncertain, and tumultuating, how roving this pretended rule is like to prove, how short it comes to any one single property of a sufficient rule, much more of all things that are necessary to complete a rule of prorocecome[2] in such cases, were easy to demonstrate. What good and useful place that is like to obtain in the worship of God, which, having its rise in the authority of man, is framed by

---

2 So the word is given in the first, and in Russell's edition. It seems a misprint for "procedure." — ED.

the rule of the wisdom of man, and so wholly resolved into his will, I may say will be one day judged and determined, but that it is so already sufficiently in the word of truth.

CHAPTER IX.

Argument second — Necessary use of the liturgy exclusive of the use of the means appointed by Christ for the edification of his church.

WE proceed to some farther considerations upon the state of the question before laid down, and shall insist on some other arguments against the imposition pleaded for. We have spoken to the authority imposing; our next argument is taken from the thing or matter imposed, and the end of that imposition.

A human provision of means for the accomplishing of any end or ends in the worship of God for which Jesus Christ himself hath made and doth continue to make provision, to the exclusion of that provision so by him made, is not allowable. About this assertion I suppose we shall have no contention. To assert the lawfulness of such provisions is, in the first instance, to exalt the wisdom and authority of men above that of Christ, and that in his own house. This men will not nakedly and openly do, though by just consequence it be done everyday. But we have secured our proposition by the plainness of its terms, against which no exception can lie. It remaineth, then, that we show that the things mentioned in it, and rejected as disallowable, are directly applicable to the imposition of liturgies contended about.

That the prescription of the liturgy, to be used as prescribed, is the provision of a means for the accomplishing of some ends in the worship of God, the judgment and the practice of those who contend for it do sufficiently declare. Those ends, or this end (to sum up all in one), is, that the ordinances and institutions of Christ may be quickly administered and solemnized in the church with decency and order, unto the edification of the assemblies wherein it is used. I suppose none will deny this to be the end intended in its imposition; it is so pleaded continually; nor is there any other that I know of assigned. Now, of the things mentioned it is the last that is the principal end, — namely, the edification of the church; which is aimed at for its own sake, and so regulates the whole procedure of mere mediums, and those that are so mediums as also to be esteemed subordinate ends. Such are decency and order, or uniformity. These have not their worth from themselves, nor do they influence the intention of the liturgists for their own sakes, but as they tend unto edification; and this he apostolical rule expressly requireth, 1 Cor. xiv. The prescription, then, of a liturgy is a provision for the right administration of the ordinances of the gospel unto the edification of the church. This is its general nature; and in the administration of the ordinances of the gospel consists the chief and main work of the ministry. That this provision is human hath been before declared. It was not made by Christ nor his apostles, but of men; and by men was it made and imposed on the disciples of Christ. It remaineth, then, that we consider whether Jesus Christ have not made provision for the same end and purpose, — namely, that the ordinances and institutions of the gospel may be administered to the edification of the church. Now, this the apostle expressly affirms, Eph. iv. 7–13, "Unto every one of us is given grace according to the measure of the gift of Christ. Wherefore he saith, When he ascended up on high, he led captivity captive, and gave gifts unto men. And he gave some, pastors and teachers; for the perfecting of the saints, for the work of the ministry, for the edifying of the body of Christ: till we all come in the unity of the faith, and of the knowledge of the Son of God, unto a perfect man, unto the measure of the stature of the fulness of Christ." The Lord Jesus, who hath appointed the office of the ministry, hath also provided sufficient furniture for the persons called according to his mind to the discharge of that office and the whole duty of it. That the administration of the ordinances of the gospel is the work of the ministry, I suppose will not be denied. Now, that this work of the ministry may be discharged to the edification of his body, and that to the end of the world, until all his people in every generation are brought unto the measure of grace assigned unto them in this life, is expressly affirmed. He hath given gifts for this end and purpose, — namely, that the work of the ministry may be performed to the edification of his body. To say that the provision he hath made is not every way sufficient for the attaining of the end for which it was made by him, or that he continueth not to make the same provision that he did formerly, are equally blasphemous; the one injurious to his wisdom, the other to his truth, both to his love and care of his church. For decency and uniformity in all his churches the Lord Jesus also hath provided. The administration of the same specifical ordinances in the assemblies of his disciples, convened according to his mind, according to the same rule of his word, by virtue of the same specifical gifts of the Spirit by him bestowed on the administrators of them, constitutes the uniformity that he requires, and is acceptable unto him. This was the uniformity of the apostolical churches, walking by the same rule of faith and obedience, and no other; and this is all the uniformity that is among the true churches of Christ that are this day in the world. To imagine that there should be a uniformity in words and phrases of speech, and the like, is an impracticable figment, which never was obtained, nor ever will be to the end of the world. And when men, by the invention of rites and orders, began to depart from this uniformity, how far they were from falling into any other is notorious from that discourse of Socrates on this matter, lib. v. cap. 21. For these, then, the Lord Christ hath made provision. And where there is this uniformity unto edification, let those things be attended unto which are requisite for the nature of assemblies meeting for such ends, as assemblies, and all the decency and order which Christ requireth will ensue. I suppose it will not be safe for any man to derogate from the sufficiency of this provision. If any shall say, that we see and find by experience that men called to be ministers are not so enabled to the work of the ministry as, by virtue of the gifts they have received, to administer the ordinances of the gospel unto the edification of the church, I shall desire them to consider whether indeed such persons be rightly called unto the ministry, and do labour aright to discharge their duty in that office; seeing that if they are so and do so, there seems to be a direct failure of the promise of Christ, which is blasphemy to imagine. And it may be considered whether this pretended defect and want do not, where it is in those who are indeed called to the work of the ministry, proceed from their neglect to stir up the gifts that they have received by the use and exercise of them; for which end alone they are intrusted with them. And it may be farther considered, whether their neglect hath not been occasioned greatly by some men's imposing of prescribed liturgies, and others trusting to their use in those things and for those ends for which men are intrusted with those gifts by Jesus Christ. And if this be so, — as indeed, upon due search, it will appear so to be, — then we have a secret inclusion of the provision made by Christ for the ends mentioned plainly intimated unto us, before we arrive at the express consideration of it.

But to proceed. The provision that Christ hath made for the discharge of the whole work of the ministry, in the administration of the ordinances of the gospel, unto the edification of his church, is his collation or bestowing of gifts on men rightly called to the office of the ministry, enabling them unto, and to be exercised in, that work. In the prescription and imposition of a liturgy, there is a provision made for the discharge of the work of the ministry, in the administration of the ordinances of the gospel, unto the edification of the church, in and by the precise reading and pronouncing of the words set down therein, without alteration, diminution, or addition. It remaineth, then, to consider whether this latter provision be not exclusive of the former, and whether the use of them both at the same time be not inconsistent. The administration of gospel ordinances consists in prayer, thanksgiving, instruction, and exhortations, suitably applied unto the special nature and end of the several ordinances themselves, and the use of them in the church. For the right performance of all these, Christ gives gifts unto ministers; the liturgy [gives] a certain number of words, to be read without addition or alteration, and this "toties quoties" as the ordinances are to be administered. Now, unless it can be made to appear that an ability to read the prescribed words of the liturgy be the gifts promised by Christ for the discharge of the work of the ministry, which cannot be done, it is most evident that there is an inconsistency between the use and actual exercise of these several provisions of mediums for the compassing of the same end; and, consequently, the necessary, indispensable use of the liturgy is directly exclusive of the use of the means provided by Christ, and for that end for which the liturgy is invented and imposed. What dismal effects have issued hereupon may be declared hereafter, if need be. Certainly more than one commandment of God, and more than one promise of Christ, have been made void by this tradition; and I desire that none would be offended if, as my own apprehension, I affirm that the introduction of liturgies was, on the account insisted on, the principal means of increasing and carrying on that sad defection and apostasy, in the guilt whereof most churches in the world have inwrapped themselves. Nor doth there lie at present any relief against this consideration from hence, that ministers are allowed the exercise of their gifts they have received in their preaching, and prayers before and after sermons. For, first, that indeed there is such a liberty allowed, if the present liturgy be so imposed as by some is pretended, is very questionable. Many that are looked on as skilled in that law and mystery of it do by their practice give another interpretation of the intendment of its imposition, making it extend to all that is done in the public worship, the bare preaching or reading of a sermon or homily excepted. Nor, secondly, is that the matter inquired into, whether ministers may at any time, or in any part of God's worship, make use of their gifts? but whether they may do it in all those administrations, for whose performance, to the edification of his body, they are bestowed on them by Jesus Christ? which, by the rule of the liturgy, we have showed they may not; and I doubt not but it will be granted, by those who contend for the imposition of the liturgy, that it extends to the principal parts, if not the whole, of the public worship of God in the church. Now, certainly, it is necessary that conscience be clearly satisfied that this prescription of a human provision of means for such ends in the worship of God as Christ hath made provision for, which is excluded thereby, be not against express rule of Scripture, Ezek. xliii. 8; Matt. xv. 9; Col. ii. 20–22; without precedent or example; derogatory to the glory of Christ, Heb. iii. 5, 6, and, in particular, of his truth, wisdom, and love of his church, as also to the perfection of the Scripture, 2 Tim. iii. 15, 16; — and whether it brings not the ministers of the gospel into open sin, Rom. xii. 6–8; 1 Cor. xii. 6–10; Eph. iv. 8, 11, 12; 1 Pet. iv. 10, 11; and so be an occasion of the wrath of God and ruin of the souls of men, before they admit of it or submit unto it.

CHAPTER X.

Other considerations about the imposition of liturgies.

FURTHERMORE, the great rule of gospel administrations is, that all things be done to edification. This is the main end of the ministry itself, in all the duties thereof that are purely evangelical. For this end was the office of the ministry instituted; for this end are ministerial gifts dispensed; for this end were the sacraments appointed, and all church assemblies, church power, and whatever else belongs to churches. It is all ordained for this end, that the body of Christ may be "edified" and "increased with the increase of God," Eph. iv. 7, 8, 11–15; Col. ii. 19; Acts ix. 31; Rom. xiv. 15, 19; 1 Cor. x. 23, xiv. 3–5, 12, 26; 2 Cor. xii. 19; 1 Tim. i. 4. The full and adequate rule of all church order and duties is, that all things be done to edification. It doth not hence ensue that whatever men shall judge to conduce to edification may be used by themselves or imposed on others in the worship of God. Christ himself, the only wise and competent judge in such cases, hath precisely himself determined what is conducing hereunto, having, as on other accounts, so on this also, limited men to his prescription, because nothing is effectual unto edification but by virtue of his blessing, which is annexed only to his own institutions. But this will undeniably hence ensue, that whatever is contrary unto or a hinderance of edification, ought not to be appointed or observed in the worship of God; for certainly whatever is a hinderance of that, in any kind, unto whose furtherance all things of that kind ought to contribute, their whole worth and virtue consisting in that contribution, can have no due place amongst them. If it appear that this is the state and condition of this imposed liturgy in church administrations, I presume it will be confessed that it ought not to obtain any place or room amongst them. The edification of the church depends principally on the blessing of God upon the exercise of those ministerial gifts which are bestowed on men for that end, — namely, that he church be edified. God supplying "seed to the sower" blesseth it with an increase in the field where it is sowed, 2 Cor. ix. 10. The gifts that are bestowed on ministers are their principal talents, that they ought to trade withal for the profit of their Master; that is, the building up of his house, wherein his wealth in this world doth lie. Yea, all the gifts that are bestowed by the Spirit of Christ on man are given them "to profit withal," 1 Cor. xii. 7; and they are required with them to act for God in the edification of the body of Christ, everyone according to his measure, 1 Pet. iv. 10, 11. This, I suppose, will be granted. Moreover, that the gifts bestowed by Christ on the guides of his church, the ministers of the gospel, are proportioned and suited to the end which he aimeth to accomplish by them, as we have in part before declared, so it is evident from the infinite wisdom of him that bestows them. From both which it will undeniably follow, that on the due and regular use and employment of those gifts which men receive from Christ depends, and that solely, the edification of his church. I suppose this will not be denied, [that] where the gifts bestowed by the Spirit of Christ upon the ministers of his church are used and exercised in the work of the ministry, according to his mind and will, there, by his blessing, the edification which he doth intend will ensue. Let us, then, proceed. These gifts, as the Scripture witnesseth and experience convinceth, are bestowed in great variety and in several degrees. The greater and more excellent they are in any intrusted with them, the more excellent is the means of edification which the Lord affords unto his disciples by them. Edification, then, as in its general nature it depends on the gifts of Christ which he bestows on the officers of his church, so as to the degrees of it and its special furtherance, it depends on the degrees and special improvement of those gifts. For this cause all those to whom the work of the ministry is committed, as they ought to "desire spiritual gifts," 1 Cor. xiv. 1, that the church may be edified by them, so to "covet earnestly the best gifts," chap. xii. 31, that they may singularly edify the church; and also seek to excel in those gifts, chap. xiv. 20, that the same word of edification may be carried on to the utmost. It may, then, be inquired how these spiritual gifts, — which we must suppose all ministers of the gospel, in some measure, to have received, — may be improved, so that they may "excel to the edifying of the church," which is expressly required of them. We say, then, that the improvement and increase of spiritual gifts doth ordinarily and regularly depend on their due and holy exercise. He that had a talent and used it not, though he endeavoured to keep it safe, yet it did not increase, when every one that traded with the stock wherewith they were intrusted made a regular increase, according to the measure they had received. And in experience we daily see men napkining their talents until they are taken from them, whilst others receive additions to their store, at least such supplies as that their first provisions fail not. Hence, the great direction for the exercise of the work of the ministry is, to stir up the gift received; by a due performance whereof, in all persons intrusted with them, is the whole work of edifying the body of Christ, until it reach the measure appointed to every member, completed and finished. Edification, then, depends on the improvement of gifts, and the improvement of gifts on their due exercise according to the mind of Christ. The want, then, of that due exercise, either by the neglect of them on whom they are bestowed, or any hinderance of it put upon them by others, is the sole way of obstructing the improvement of spiritual gifts, and, by direct and immediate consequence, of the edification of the church. Now, this seems to be so much done by the prescription of the liturgy and imposition of it, that it is impossible for the wit of man to invent a more effectual expedient for the compassing of that evil end. The main exercise of spiritual gifts, on which their growth and improvement doth depend, lies in the administration of gospel ordinances; that is, the work of the ministry, for which they are bestowed. To hinder, therefore, or forbid that exercise is directly to forbid the due, regular, appointed means of their increase; and so, also, of the edification of the body of Christ, the means indispensably necessary unto it being removed and taken away. Now, this is open and avowedly done in the imposed liturgy, if imposed. It says expressly that the ministers of the gospel shall not use or exercise any spiritual gift in the administration of those ordinances for which provision is made in the book.

And as in this case the condition of the people, who are deprived of the means of their edification, is sad, so that of the ministers of the gospel is miserable and deplorable. The Lord Jesus Christ bestows gifts upon them, requiring the use and exercise of them in the work of the ministry at their utmost peril; men, on the other side, forbid them that use and exercise, and that with such forcible prohibitions as threaten to bear down the whole public exercise of the ministry before them. But the Lord knows how to deliver those that are his out of temptation. It will be no relief against the force of this consideration, that there are some things left wherein ministers may exercise their gifts and trade with their talents; for as this is but pretended, so it is not in this or that part of their work, but in the whole of the ministry committed unto them, that Christ indispensably requires the guides of his church that they should trade with their talents and exercise their gifts; and accordingly are they to provide for their account at the last day. By this one engine, then, at the same time, are the people deprived of the means of edification provided for them in the care, wisdom, and love of the Lord Christ, and ministers brought into a necessity of sinning, or foregoing the public exercise of their ministry.

Again, in particular, it is the work and duty of the ministers of the gospel to make application of the grace of Christ, whereof they are stewards, to the flocks committed to their charge, and that according to the especial state and condition of all especial wants which may any way be known unto them. The way of their application of this grace lies principally in the administration of gospel ordinances. Therein are they to declare, unfold, tender, and apply the grace of Christ, according unto the wants of his disciples, the good of whose souls they watch for in particular. These wants are very far from being the same, in the same degree, in and unto every congregation, or unto any one congregation at all times, or unto all persons in any congregation; which is easily discerned by a faithful and skilful guide. The especial application, then, mentioned, according to the rule of the gospel, and special addresses unto God in the name of the flock, with respect to the especial wants of all or any of them, belong to that edification which Christ hath appointed for his church. Now, how this duty can be attended unto in the observance of a prescribed form of liturgy, from whence it is not lawful to digress, is beyond my understanding to apprehend. I confess, men who scoff at edification and deride spiritual gifts, who think all religion to consist in the observation of some carnal institution, who neither know nor care to come to an acquaintance with the spiritual wants of poor souls, nor do tremble at the threatenings of Christ pointed against their negligence and ignorance, Ezek. xxxiv. 4; that suppose the whole baptized world converted to God, and preaching itself, on that account, less necessary than formerly at the first plantation of the gospel; that esteem the doubts and temptations of believers as needless scruples, and their sedulous endeavours to grow in grace and the knowledge of our Lord Jesus Christ, labour lost in hypocrisy; that perhaps do envy at and are troubled with the light and knowledge of the people of God, and suppose they can discharge the duty of the ministry by a bare reading of the service-book to their parish, by themselves, or some hired by them so to do, without once inquiring into the spiritual condition of them the care of whose souls they plead to be committed to them, — may think light of this consideration: but those who know the terror of the Lord, and any thing of their own duty, will be otherwise minded. Yea, farther, there seems to be in the imposition of a liturgy, to be used always as a form in all gospel administrations, an unwarrantable abridgment of the liberty wherewith Christ hath made us free, and therefore sin in the imposition and use of it; for as it is a sin in others to abridge us of the liberty purchased for us by Jesus Christ, so it is in us to give it up, and not to suffer in our testimony for it. Now, of that liberty purchased for us by Jesus Christ, so far as it relates to the worship of God, there are two parts, — first, A freedom from those pedagogical institutions of God himself, which by his own appointment were to continue only to the time of reformation; secondly, A freedom from subjection to the authority of men as to any new impositions in or about the worship of God, 1 Cor. vii. 23. And the same rule is given out as to our duty and deportment in reference unto both these, Gal. v. 1; 1 Pet. ii. 16. Now, not to stand fast in the liberty for us purchased by Christ, is not to have that esteem of it as a privilege given us by his love we ought to have, nor that sense of it as a duty enjoined us by him which ought to be in us. I say, there is the same reason of both these in respect of liberty. As we are freed from Mosaical institutions, so that none can impose the observation of them upon us by virtue of their first appointment, so are we also from any succeeding impositions of men. Our liberty equally respects the one and the other. And as to those institutions, such was the tenderness of the Holy Ghost and the apostles of our Lord Jesus Christ, by his directions and guidance, that they would not (no, not for a season) enjoin the observance of any of them (no, not of those which put men on no positive duties, but were mere abridgments in point of some practices) upon the disciples of Christ, but only such whose observation for that season was made necessary by reason of scandals and offences before any such imposition of theirs, Acts xv. Nor, by a parity of reason, if regard be had to their example, can there any abridgment be lawfully made of the liberty of Christ's disciples by any imposition of things of the latter sort, unless it be as to the observation of some such things as are made necessary in case of scandal antecedent unto any such imposition. We grant, then, that there may be, yea, there ought "de facto" to be, an abridgment made of our liberty as to the performance of some things at some times, which in general we are made free unto, where that performance, in the use and exercise of our liberty, would prove a hinderance unto edification, the great end whereunto all these things are subservient. But then the case must be so stated antecedent to any imposition. First to impose that which is not necessary, and then to assert a necessity of its observation lest scandal should ensue, is a course that men are not directed unto by any gospel rule or apostolical practice. The sum is, That abridgment of the liberty of the disciples of Christ, by impositions on them of things which he hath not appointed, nor made necessary by circumstances antecedent unto such impositions, are plain usurpations upon the consciences of the disciples of Christ, destructive of the liberty which he hath purchased for them, and which, if it be their duty to walk according to gospel rule, is sinful to submit unto. That of this nature is the imposition of a liturgy contended about is evident. It hath no institution or appointment by Jesus Christ, it is wholly of men; there is nothing antecedent unto its imposition that should make it necessary to be imposed; a necessity of its observation is induced upon and by its imposition, which is directly destructive to our liberty in Jesus Christ. The necessity pretended from the insufficiency of ministers for the discharge of that which is their proper work hath in great part been caused by this imposition, and where it hath not, some men's sin is not to be made other men's punishment. Reasons pleaded for the imposition opposed shall be elsewhere considered.

www.ingramcontent.com/pod-product-compliance
Lightning Source LLC
Chambersburg PA
CBHW011316080526
44587CB00024B/4014